How to use E

In this issue

The 91 daily readings in this issue of *Explore* are designed to help you understand and apply the Bible as you read it each day.

It's serious!

We suggest that you allow 15 minutes each day to work through the Bible passage with the notes. It should be a meal, not a snack! Readings from other parts of the Bible can throw valuable light on the study passage. These cross-references can be skipped if you are already feeling full up, but will expand your grasp of the Bible. *Explore* uses the NIV2011 Bible translation, but you can also use it with the NIV1984 or ESV translations.

Sometimes a prayer box will encourage you to stop and pray through the lessons—but it is always important to allow time to pray for God's Spirit to bring his word to life, and to shape the way we think and live through it.

We're serious!

All of us who work on Explore share a passion for getting the Bible into people's lives. We fiercely hold to the Bible as God's word— to honour and follow, not to explain away.

1 Find a time you can read the Bible each day

2 Find a place where you can be quiet and think

3 Ask God to help you understand

4 Carefully read through the Bible passage for today

5 Study the verses with Explore, taking time to think

6 Pray about what you have read

thegoodbook COMPANY

Opening up the Bible

Welcome to Explore

Being a Christian isn't a skill you learn, like carpentry or flower arranging. Nor is it a lifestyle choice, like the kind of clothes you wear, or the people you choose to hang out with. It's about having a real relationship with the living God through his Son, Jesus Christ. The Bible tells us that this relationship is like a marriage.

It's important to start with this, because many Christians view the practice of daily Bible-reading as a Christian duty, or a hard discipline that is just one more thing to get done in our busy modern lives.

But the Bible is God speaking to us: opening his mind to us on how he thinks, what he wants for us and what his plans are for the world. And most importantly, it tells us what he has done for us in sending his Son, Jesus Christ, into the world. It's the way the Spirit shows Jesus to us, and changes us as we behold his glory.

The Bible is not a manual. It's a love letter. And as with any love letter, we'll want to treasure it, and make time to read and re-read it, so we know we are loved, and discover how we can please the One who loves us. Here are a few suggestions for making your daily time with God more of a joy than a burden:

- *Time:* Find a time when you will not be disturbed, and when the cobwebs are cleared from your mind. Many people have found that the morning is the best time as it sets you up for the day. If you're not a "morning person", then last thing at night or a mid-morning break might suit you. Whatever works for you is right for you.

- *Place:* Jesus says that we are not to make a great show of our religion *(see Matthew 6:5-6)*, but rather, to pray with the door to our room shut. Some people plan to get to work a few minutes earlier and get their Bible out in an office or some other quiet corner.

- *Prayer:* Although *Explore* helps with specific prayer ideas from the passage, try to develop your own lists to pray through. Use the flap inside the back cover to help with this. And allow what you read in the Scriptures to shape what you pray for yourself, the world and others.

- *Share:* As the saying goes: *expression deepens impression.* So try to cultivate the habit of sharing with others what you have learned. Why not join our Facebook group to share your encouragements, questions and prayer requests? Search for *Explore: For your daily walk with God.*

And remember, *it's quality, not quantity, that counts:* better to think briefly about a single verse than to skim through pages without absorbing anything, because it's about developing your relationship with the living God. The sign that your daily time with God is real is when you start to love him more and serve him more wholeheartedly.

Tim Thornborough and Carl Laferton
Editors

ACTS: Encouragements

We are rejoining Paul in the book of Acts, for the final stage in our journey through this wonderful record of the start of our risen Lord's work in and through his church.

The story so far

To begin with, let's remind ourselves of how we reached this point in the book.

❓ *Read Acts 1:7-8. What mission did the risen Jesus give his followers?*

❓ *Read Acts 2:1-14. How was the church empowered to begin this mission?*

❓ *Read Acts 7:54 – 8:8. What caused the believers to leave Jerusalem, and what effect did that have on the spread of the gospel?*

In Acts 9, Saul (Paul) is miraculously converted on the road to Damascus, and the Lord identifies him as "my chosen instrument to proclaim my name to the Gentiles" (9:15). In Acts 10, God shows Peter that the gospel is indeed for Gentiles, who can be saved by faith in Christ in just the same way as Jews must be.

❓ *Scan-read Acts 16 – 19. In which cities did the Spirit work through Paul to plant new churches of believers?*

❓ *What kinds of opposition did the messengers of the gospel face?*

The journey continues

Read Acts 20:1-6

❓ *What does Paul do after he leaves Ephesus, and why (v 1-3)?*

Chronology is important in the book of Acts because it demonstrates God's sovereign plan for the world as it unfolds through the lives of the apostles. Using Paul's letters to the Corinthians, we can work out that Paul most likely left Ephesus in May of AD 55.

He is accompanied by many emerging leaders in the church. The names and locations listed in verse 4 demonstrate the incredible spread of the gospel out of Jerusalem and Antioch throughout all Asia Minor, including Galatia, and beyond into Macedonia and Greece. Luke also accompanies Paul.

Those listed in verse 4 went ahead of Paul and Luke with the intention of reuniting with them in Troas. The smaller party sailed out of Philippi toward Troas. The mention of seemingly minor details like times and locations bolsters the historicity of the book. Luke does the work of a historian as he laces his narrative together with the geographic progress of Paul's mission.

◪ Pray

Consider the advance of the gospel from Acts 1 (about 120 believers in a single city) to Acts 20 (dozens of churches throughout the eastern Mediterranean). Thank God that he oversees his plans to bring them to fruition and uses his people to bring those purposes about. Recommit yourself to the ongoing mission to bring the gospel "to the ends of the earth". Ask the Lord to show you how you can utilise your time, friendships, hobbies and money to that end.

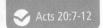
A dangerous sermon

This passage could be seen as a warning against long-winded preaching! But it is, in fact, a pointer to something much greater than that.

A long sermon

Read Acts 20:7-9

Verse 7 marks the first mention in the New Testament of Christian worship on the first day of the week—on what we call Sunday. Christians shifted their day of worship from the Jewish Sabbath to the Lord's Day to commemorate the resurrection of the Lord Jesus Christ.

❓ *For how long does Paul speak to the church in Troas?*

❓ *What effect does this have on Eutychus, and with what tragic result (v 9)?*

A great resurrection

Read Acts 20:10-12

❓ *What does Paul do, and with what result (v 10)?*

❓ *What does he then resume doing (v 11)?!*

There are only seven cases in the whole Bible, apart from the resurrection of Jesus (and those mentioned in Matthew 27 v 52), where human beings are raised from the dead. There are two in the Old Testament, when Elijah and Elisha raise individuals from the dead. Jesus himself raises three people, to show his own authority over death: Jairus's daughter, the young man of Nain, and Lazarus. Two apostles, by the Spirit's power, also raise the dead to life. The first is Peter, who saw Dorcas return to life (Acts 9:36-41). The second is Paul here.

Read 1 Kings 17:17-24; 2 Kings 4:32-37

❓ *What similarities do you see between the way the Lord worked through Elijah and Elisha, and through Paul here in Acts 20?*

Notice that God worked through Elijah in such a way to prove that he was a true man of God: a prophet whose words must be listened to. In a similar way, God worked through Paul so that the church (today as well as then) would know that his words must be listened to—as the church in Troas continued to do after Eutychus was raised (Acts 20:11).

So what are we to make of this today? This narrative should call us to the power of the gospel and the preaching of the Lord Jesus Christ. This was not a miracle service interrupted by a word of preaching. This was preaching interrupted by a miracle. Though no Christian today should expect to experience what Eutychus did, every Christian will experience more than he did. One day, Christ will raise us all up from the grave, and on that day we will be brought back to an eternal life.

⌃ Pray

Thank God for the greater miracle he wrought in your heart when you first believed the word of the gospel; and for the resurrection you will one day experience.

Paul's leadership school

The time has come for Paul to say his farewell to the Ephesians. So he calls the elders of that church to Miletus, some 80 kilometres from Ephesus.

Read Acts 20:13-21

Leaders train leaders

❓ *Why did the elders need to travel to Miletus, rather than Paul detouring to Ephesus itself?*

Perhaps more notable than Paul summoning the elders to make this journey is that Paul prioritised speaking with them at all, given the hurry he was in. But a leader's time is never wasted in developing other leaders. Paul ensures his legacy will continue through the faithful leadership of well-equipped and trained elders who will preach the word of God and proclaim the excellencies of Christ to the people of the region.

Leaders teach the gospel

❓ *What did Paul's ministry in Ephesus comprise (v 18-21)?*

This breaks down into three core activities:

1. *Serving the Lord in humility.* Paul's style of leadership provides a helpful and desperately needed paradigm for the 21st century. Leading in ministry does involve back-room vision-casting and executive management. Leadership is not less than that, but it is also more. Ministry also consists of service, teaching the saints and putting the fame of Christ first. In essence, Christian ministry must be about Jesus and about people, and not about the minister.

2. *Boldly teaching all that is helpful.* Christianity suffers from too many churches that preach a half-gospel, which is no gospel at all. Pastors must be willing to imitate Paul by standing upon the sure and lasting rock of the infallible word of God, and not failing to "preach anything that would be helpful" (v 20).

3. *Preaching the gospel of repentance and faith to all.* Paul preached the exact same message to both Jews and Gentiles. There is one gospel by which we are saved (Acts 4:12; Romans 1:16). He does not modify the content of his message to suit the preferences or sensibilities of his audience, but preaches the full gospel of repentance and faith.

⌄ Apply

Think about any ministry you are involved in—whether it be pulpit preaching, eldership, small-group leading, or children's work, and so on.

❓ *What would it look like for you to serve those in your care by working as Paul had laboured in Ephesus? Does anything need to change in your approach?*

⌃ Pray

❓ *How does this passage prompt you to give thanks for, and pray for, your pastor(s)?*

Do so now.

Keep watch

There is great emotion in Paul's speech to these elders—because he knows he will not return to them. His return to Jerusalem will culminate in imprisonment.

We must read these words in that context.

Read Acts 20:22-31

Towards trouble

❓ *What does Paul know (v 23)?*
❓ *So why does Paul not turn back (v 24)?*

Jerusalem had been the birthplace of the church, but it was now home to the rejection of the gospel. To proclaim the name of Christ in Jerusalem was tantamount to signing your own death sentence. Paul, however, does not press towards Jerusalem in order to self-destruct. He feels bound by the Spirit. Paul measures the worth of his life by whatever purpose God will use it for.

Innocent of blood

❓ *What does Paul declare (v 26-27)?*

In Ezekiel 33:1–7, the Lord tells Ezekiel that he will serve as a watchman who will speak the oracles of God to warn the people. If the watchman speaks and the people do not listen to the warning, their blood will be upon the people's hands. If the watchman does not speak, however, and the people are killed, their blood is on the watchman's hands. Paul has no blood on his hands because he has not failed, everywhere he has gone, to preach the gospel. Paul can say that he is innocent of blood because he "did not shrink from declaring to you the whole counsel of God" (Acts 20:27, ESV).

Apply

❓ *Some preaching is not "innocent of ... blood". Can you think of any examples that you have come across?*
❓ *Which parts of the "whole counsel of God"—that is, everything God has said to us in his word—are you most tempted not to speak of?*
❓ *How does this idea of being "innocent of ... blood" spur you to action today? With whom is the Spirit prompting you to share the gospel?*

Watch out for wolves

❓ *What does Paul command, and why (v 28-30)?*
❓ *How would this charge feel all the more urgent, given his understanding that none of them "will ever see [him] again"?*

"Savage wolves" (v 29) are external threats to the church. Their attempts to annihilate the church will not be subtle ones. The other threat is more insidious and harder to spot—an internal threat of false teaching that subtly works to lead sheep astray. So elders need to "keep watch" (v 28).

Pray

Pray for your own church leaders—that they will lead you sacrificially and be careful to teach truth and defend the flock against attack and error, wherever it may arise.

The word of his grace

We need to recognise humanity's inability to produce supernatural results. Effective ministry relies on God's grace, rests on God's word, and works hard in his strength.

Final words

Read Acts 20:32-35

❓ *What is "the word of [God's] grace" able to do (v 32)?*

❓ *What kind of church leader was Paul (v 33-35)?*

Paul didn't preach this gospel for selfish gain or ambition. He was controlled by one reality: the glory of God. This is not to say that ministers of the gospel should not be paid. Paul spills considerable ink elsewhere in defending his right to receive support from the church (1 Corinthians 9:14; 1 Timothy 5:17-18). What he does here is to contrast himself with some of the false teachers operating throughout Macedonia and Asia who preached for selfish gain. Paul worked for his own money. Moreover, he worked outside of ministry so that he might have something to give to the needy (v 35).

☑ Apply

❓ *Where would sticking up the words "It is more blessed to give than receive" help you to treat others as Paul did? On your work computer? On the inside of your front door? Above your kitchen sink?*

Last goodbyes

Read Acts 20:36-38

❓ *How did the people involved feel as they said their farewells, and why?*

Paul's impact on this church's life cannot be overstated, and the affections they had for him are demonstrable proof of that. Caring for the flock is straining work, but a pastor who endeavours to minister in the pattern of Paul can enjoy an equal measure of affection and admiration. More importantly, and by God's grace alone, the pastor who longs to minister as Paul ministered will not have worked in vain, and can look forward to walking into the celestial gathering and hearing those resplendent words, "Well done, my good and faithful servant".

☑ Apply

Think about any areas of Christian service or leadership you are involved in, be it in the home or the church, or elsewhere. Now, with those roles in mind, flick your eyes over verses 18-35.

❓ *What particularly challenges you in your own ministries as you read them?*

❓ *What verse do you need to memorise?*

❓ *How does verse 32 encourage you to keep working hard in ministering with "the word of grace" to others today?*

◪ Pray

Pray for your pastor(s), that they would care for your church as Paul cared for the Ephesian one. Pray for opportunities actively to encourage them about ways they are doing this.

Bible in a year: Leviticus 4-5 • Hebrews 7 ✔

Don't go... must go

Paul's ministry now takes on a different character as his third missionary journey ends and the final phase of his life begins. Paul is on his way to Jerusalem—or is he?

Urged not to go

Read Acts 21:1-6

❓ *What do the disciples in Tyre say to Paul (v 4)?*
❓ *To what extent does Paul listen to them (v 5-6)?*

We already know that the Spirit is leading Paul to Jerusalem (20:22-23), and now these Christians seem to be proclaiming a different message from the Spirit. Is the Spirit contradicting himself? No. The Holy Spirit revealed Paul's future destiny of arrest and suffering to these Christians, just as he had to Paul. Based on this revelation, they attempted to persuade Paul to avoid suffering—and, inadvertently, encouraged Paul to oppose the Spirit's leading. Paul, though, committed himself to the will of God and the leading of the Spirit—even if that was to lead him into trials.

Urged not to go (again)

Read Acts 21:7-16

In the early church, prophecy took two forms—both are found in this passage.

First, prophecy could function as evangelism. Oftentimes, the act of teaching or sharing the gospel was referred to as prophesying. This form of prophecy fits best with Philip's daughters. Philip is referred to as the evangelist (v 8), and his daughters most likely followed him in that role.

Second, prophecy was a literal prediction concerning near-future events. This is seen most clearly in the character of Agabus.

❓ *What does Agabus prophesy (v 11)?*
❓ *How do Paul's companions now echo the sentiments of the believers in Tyre (v 12)?*
❓ *To what extent does Paul listen to them (v 13-14)?*

We can learn something revolutionary from Paul. Though fully aware of the impending suffering to befall him, he did not hesitate to continue his mission. Paul's chief concern in life was not comfort, safety or a long life. It was the proclamation of the gospel of God, no matter the cost. God summons all his people to trust perfectly in his will. Indeed, Pauls' sufferings bore tremendous fruit as his tribulations often resulted in the advancement of the kingdom of God. For us as for him, the question should not be "Why does suffering happen to me?" but rather, "How can I proclaim the gospel of Jesus in the midst of my trials?"

▼ Apply

❓ *In what way do you need to hear these truths about suffering and trials today? What might the answer be to that question at the end of the section above?*

PROVERBS: Family values

We're taking a break from Psalms on Sundays to spend some time in Proverbs. The nuggets of wisdom in these chapters are best thought about slowly and carefully.

We're born into a web of relationships that we call family, community, nationality and humanity. But we feel the connection with family most keenly.

Read Proverbs 1:1-2, 7

❓ *How are the words "wisdom" and "fools" used here? What meaning do the words convey?*

Read Proverbs 10:1

❓ *What powerful truth is expressed by this verse?*

❓ *Have you experienced this yourself— either as a child to your parent(s) or as a parent yourself? Or have you seen it in another family you know?*

❓ *What opposite effects are contrasted in this verse?*

Many of the one-line proverbs that make up most of Proverbs 10 – 31 can seem like just "worldly wisdom"—how to get along and prosper in the world. But they are so much more than that. The knowledge of God and worshipful respect for him, his creation and others are at the heart of the way of wisdom. Truly wise people act in the wise ways that they do because they know and fear the LORD. Foolish people act as they do because, in their hearts, they say, "There is no God" (Psalm 53:1). And godly parents will be delighted when they see wisdom in their kids, and will be downcast when they are foolish. That doesn't mean being proud that they have got a first-class degree or ashamed that they crashed out of education with no qualifications—because that's not wisdom or foolishness. Christian parents are most delighted by their children knowing God, and the children showing signs of wisdom in their lives—in the way they think, live and relate to others in very practical ways.

Our *greatest* joy should be reserved for those times when we see a child who follows Jesus wholeheartedly—and our greatest grief for those who live with no reference to God in the world.

⌄ Apply

It's so very easy for parents to take pride in the wrong things.

❓ *Has this infected the way you think about your children, or the families you are connected to?*

❓ *How can you subtly (or unsubtly!) challenge that thinking when you hear it from others?*

⌃ Pray

Pray for the families at your church: that parents would know the joy of seeing their children walk in God's ways. Pray for any children you know who do not walk with the Lord. Ask God to turn their parents' grief to joy.

Freedom and the gospel

After an absence of about five years, Paul arrives in Jerusalem. It is (at first) a very encouraging time.

Read Acts 21:17-20

❷ *How is Paul able to encourage James and the elders of the Jerusalem church?*
❷ *How are they able to encourage Paul?*

Don't miss the significance of "They praised God" (v 20). Only the gospel could bridge the gap—the ethnic divide—between Jews and Gentiles. Only the gospel can tear down the divides which exist in our own day.

Read Acts 21:21-26

❷ *What do the elders ask Paul to do, and why (v 20-24)?*
❷ *How does Paul respond (v 26)?*
❷ *Does this surprise you? Why/why not?*

Many Jews believed that Paul was teaching antinomianism—that he wanted to abolish the law of Moses (v 21). This misunderstanding threatened to cause a fissure in the already fragile bonds between Jews and Gentiles.

The relationship between a Christ-following Jew and Jewish law is, biblically, a complicated issue. On the one hand, the Jewish believer cannot find salvation in the Jewish traditions. On the other hand, Scripture does not forbid a Jew to give up his practice of Jewish customs. He can assimilate to the lifestyle of the Gentiles while having a respect for where he has come from. He can also continue in Jewish customs but with the understanding that salvation comes through Christ and Christ alone.

The Jerusalem elders, therefore, cautiously wanted to keep the gospel at the forefront of these Jews' lives while respecting their individual consciences.

Verse 23 probably has in view the Nazirite vow of Numbers 6:1-13. A Nazirite would pursue a purified, holy lifestyle of singular devotion to God. This meant avoiding wine, dead bodies, and anything unclean.

Paul could have refused the request to join in with these rites. Instead he submitted himself to the elders' request because his priority was maintaining the character of the gospel while also promoting the unity of the church. He did not want to leave an obstacle between the gospel and the Jews. The gospel cannot change but our presentation of it, at times, must (1 Corinthians 9:22).

☑ Apply

Paul is showing us something astounding about true freedom. In Galatians 5:1, Paul exclaimed, "It is for freedom that Christ has set us free!" Believers, however, can let freedom rise to the status of an idol and, consequently, enslave themselves to freedom. True freedom means Christians can dispense with their own preferences, wants and needs. True freedom is a freedom from self: a freedom to lay down our freedoms as a sacrifice on the altar of Christian love.

❷ *What drives you more—what you're free to do, or what is loving to others?*

The apostle and the mob

Paul had taken part in the purification of Nazirite men to show that he still took the Jewish law with due seriousness. It did not work…

The accusation
Read Acts 21:27-29

❓ *Who accused Paul (v 27-28)? Of what?*
❓ *Was the charge fair (v 29)?*

The inner sanctuary was off-limits to non-Jews. Paul knew not to bring a Gentile into the temple, and had not done so. The accusation, however, was enough to ensure a violent riot...

In the hands of the mob
Read Acts 21:30-36

❓ *Why is Paul not killed by the mob (v 31-32)?*
❓ *What state does Paul finish up in (v 33-36)?*
❓ *How does this fulfil the prophecy given through Agabus (v 10-11)?*

···· TIME OUT ·········

Read Romans 9:1-4; 10:1

❓ *What do these verses tell us about how Paul felt about the mob who were trying to kill him?*

Pray now that you would have this same loving desire for those around you—even if they mock your faith or actively oppose it.

In the hands of the commander
Read Acts 21:37-40

The commander was surprised to hear Paul speak in Greek (v 37), and then he assumed that Paul was the Egyptian perpetrator of a revolt in the Judean wilderness in AD 54 (v 38). Paul responded by identifying himself as a Jew from Tarsus. Then he made a request. He desired to speak to the mob who had just attempted to kill him (v 39). The tribune gave him permission, and so Paul walked back out to face the crowd and give a speech that would certainly not be forgotten. But for the moment, mark his courage. This was the courage of a man who knew that, whatever may happen, all was under the sovereign hand of his Lord.

🔽 Apply
❓ *What would change in how you speak, and who you speak to, if you had the same love and courage today that Paul did on that day?*

🔼 Pray
Pray now that you would live and speak as Paul did. And pray specifically for those you long to evangelise (especially if you know you have been avoiding opportunities to speak to them of Christ out of fear of mockery, rejection, or some other cost).

Before and after

"After receiving the commander's permission, Paul stood on the steps and motioned to the crowd. When they were all silent, he said to them…" (Acts 21:40)

Zealous Jew

Read Acts 22:1-5

❓ *In what ways does Paul establish that he is committed to furthering the cause of Jewish religion?*

If Paul were to stop his speech at this point, the crowd would applaud. Paul, however, no longer roots his life in his ethnic identity, education or work. Something powerful and transformative had gripped Paul as he travelled on the road to Damascus to persecute Christians (v 5).

Wonderful conversion

Read Acts 22:6-16

Paul is recounting his experience, which Luke has already told us of in Acts 9. There is an irony in 22:9. As the arresting party in Acts 9 saw the light but could not understand, so too does the mob in front of Paul now see the light of the gospel, but fails to understand its saving power.

❓ *What did Ananias tell Paul about God's purposes for him (v 14-16)?*

Committed Christian

Read Acts 22:17-21

❓ *What doubts does Paul have about his ability to minister effectively in Christ's cause (v 19-20)?*
❓ *How does the Lord respond (v 21)?*

Apply

Paul's inclusion in his testimony of his life outside of grace should encourage us to reflect on our own lives before we came to Christ. If we came to faith at a point we can remember, we can look back on a previous life of total sin and rebellion. This should stir up gratitude and thanksgiving. Only as we acknowledge the depth of our sin can we appreciate the glory of our conversion (1 Timothy 1:15).

❓ *What is your story? Do you tend to sugarcoat the nature and depth of your pre-conversion rebellion, or do you risk making it sound exciting and attractive?*
❓ *How can you speak of your "before" and "after" in such a way that both bring Christ glory?*

Pray

Though our lives will surely not have the global impact of Paul's, our stories also parallel Paul's testimony. We too have been saved by God out of our sin, rebellion and disobedience. God longs for his people to demonstrate the transformative power of the gospel through baptism and evangelism.

Ask God to direct you, today, to someone who will be receptive to your story and to the gospel that saved you.

Until he said this...

Up to this point, the Jewish mob, though they may be annoyed, have not reacted aggressively against Paul. The last sentence of his speech, however, tips the scales.

What angered the mob

Read Acts 22:21-22

❓ *What is it that so angers the mob?*

The Jews could not stomach this thought because they reviled the Gentiles. They viewed the Gentiles as defilers of the temple and as harsh overlords. The Jews in Jerusalem repudiated Gentile rule of their holy city of David. And now Paul tells them that Yahweh, the God of Israel, has had the audacity to graft the Gentiles into the family of God.

It is easy to change or downplay parts of God's revelation to make the message of the gospel less offensive. The gospel, however, is offensive. In Acts 17, Paul knew he would lose many in his audience by speaking of the resurrection from the dead. Here in Acts 22, Paul knew he would illicit a strong response from the Jews by proclaiming the inclusion of Gentiles in the kingdom of God. Paul could have left out the points which caused so much hostility and mockery from the crowds. For Paul to do that, however, would have meant him capitulating on the central doctrines of the gospel and their implications. He would have been attempting to shape God to the culture rather than summoning the culture to turn to God. The idea of conforming the gospel to the cultural streams remains tempting. It might lead to less suffering and mockery. To do this, however, would mean jettisoning the message of salvation. If your desire for cultural relevance supersedes the theological commitments of the Christian faith, then you will not preach good news, though you may proclaim culturally popular news.

What protected Paul

Read Acts 22:23-29

❓ *Why is Paul not flogged (v 25-29)?*

The answer to Paul's question in verse 25 is "No". The protection of Caesar extended to every citizen of the Roman Empire. Notice that while Paul trusted in the will of God and would endure any suffering which befell him, he did not pursue unnecessary suffering. Suffering for the sake of suffering does not glorify God. Paul used his citizenship as a protection, not because he feared suffering, but rather as a gift of God in order to continue to advance the gospel.

☑ Apply

❓ *Are you willing to risk offence in order to proclaim the gospel clearly?*
❓ *Which parts does your particular culture request or demand that you leave out?*
❓ *Are there positions or privileges you enjoy that you could use to give yourself a platform for sharing the gospel? What are those, and how could they be used?*

Resurrection division

The Roman commander is now thoroughly confused—so he sends Paul to the Sanhedrin, the same priestly court that condemned the Lord to death.

Paul and the high priest

Read Acts 22:30 – 23:5

> ❷ *What does Paul say to the high priest (v 3)?*
> ❷ *What do you make of his response to realising who he has insulted (v 4-5)?*

When we are presented with a difficult interpretive decision, oftentimes the simplest explanation offers the safest route. Most likely, Paul did lose his temper here, lashing out in a moment of frustration. As soon as he was told who he had addressed, Paul offered an apology, grounding his confession not in the character of Ananias but in the Old Testament Scriptures.

⌄ Apply

There is nothing Christian about refusing to accept we are in error. It does not undermine our witness to acknowledge that we are human and do make mistakes.

> ❷ *How quick are you to accept you've made a mistake, and how quick are you to unreservedly apologise?*

Pharisees and Sadducees

Read Acts 23:6-10

Paul now masterfully redirects proceedings.

> ❷ *What does he know (v 6)?*
> ❷ *What did these two groups of Jewish religious leaders disagree about (v 8)?*

> ❷ *What was Paul's purpose in saying what he did in verse 6, do you think?*
> ❷ *Did it work (v 7, 9-10)?*

Many opponents of Christianity today highlight the innumerable denominations which exist in the church. The charge goes, "How can Christians lay any claim to the truth if they themselves have divided so many times and cannot present a united message?" This scene is a reminder that opponents of Christianity disagree on issues of truth within their own camps too. The charge can easily be turned back on those who so confidently level it at Christianity.

Left to itself, humanity will never think and act in ways that accord with the truth. Only through God's grace and God's revelation—which comes from outside of humanity and was incarnated in humanity—can humanity know and live out the truth.

Acts 23 reminds us that God often flips the script on our expectations. Like Jesus standing before the authorities in the Gospels, the interrogated one becomes the interrogator. The Sanhedrin will not judge Paul; God will judge the Sanhedrin. The next chapters will show that nobody judges the gospel—it is the gospel which judges us.

⌄ Apply

> ❷ *How do the truths in this passage give you confidence as you seek to obey and share the gospel?*

To Rome

The next night Paul—alone, unsure of his future and perhaps entertaining thoughts of fear and anxiety—is visited by the Lord.

The Lord comes

Read Acts 23:11

❷ *What is Paul to do? What path will he walk?*

Notice the intimate language. The Lord came and "stood" by Paul, speaking words of comfort, and shared with Paul the will of God. God was not done with him. Paul had more to proclaim and more people with whom to share the gospel. Paul needed not only comfort but courage: the courage only God can supply. We need that same courage today. When pressed with doubts, fears and anxiety, grab hold of God and do not let go. Plead with him for courage and strength.

⌃ Pray

Ask God for this kind of courage now.

The apostle goes

Verse 11 sets the direction for the rest of Acts. God has revealed to Paul that he intends Paul should go to Rome and present the gospel there. Thus, the rest of the narrative will demonstrate God's faithfulness in carrying Paul through various trials to his final destination. The story will also highlight how Paul continues to press on in faithfulness, and maintains his courage as he trusts in God and his promise.

Read Acts 23:12-35

❷ *What are the Jews plotting (v 12-15)?*

❷ *How are their plans foiled (v 16-24)?*
❷ *To what extent is the commander's letter true (v 27-30)?*

Luke contrasts the self-serving soldier and his half-truthful letter with the Christ-exalting apostle and his fully truthful testimony.

❷ *Where does Paul end up (v 33, 35)?*

The Jewish plot did not surprise God. He knew exactly what would happen and, before they even hatched their plot, had already curtailed their efforts. God's providential protection continually guides Paul along his journey to Rome. The road of God's providence may contain much difficulty, but we go with God. The path of discipleship will come with pangs and sorrow, trials and suffering, but it is a glorious way, and we know our destination—not Rome but the celestial city. God has pulled back the curtain of eternity and shown his children the celestial gathering that awaits us. So, like Paul, we can live courageously and strive obediently, for we know where we are heading, and that the Lord will bring us there.

⌄ Apply

❷ *What difference does this need to make to the way you look at:*
- *your disappointments?*
- *things that make you fearful?*
- *things that make you joyful?*

We'll rejoin Paul after we've enjoyed focusing on Easter for the next nine days.

EASTER: Betrayal & love

This Easter in Explore, we're in the final three chapters of Matthew's Gospel. We pick up the story in chapter 26: "When Jesus had finished saying all these things…"

Those "things" are the contents of chapters 23 – 25, the last of five big blocks of Jesus' teaching in this Gospel. 26:1 signals that the time for teaching is now "finished"—Jesus has said all he needs to say. Now, in the Gospel's dramatic climax, we'll see Jesus do all he needs to do: die and rise again.

Read Matthew 26:1-5

❓ *What is significant about Jesus' statement in verse 2, and what we're told in verses 3-5? (What is Matthew trying to draw our attention to by writing it like this, do you think?)*

❓ *What dilemma do the chief priests and elders face? What's their proposed solution?*

This is a theme we'll see repeated in the chapters that follow. Jesus knows what is going to happen to him and is in total control of the action.

Read Matthew 26:6-13

❓ *What surprising turn does this dinner party take (v 6-7)?*

❓ *Who is angry, and why (v 8-9)? Does this seem reasonable?*

❓ *What does Jesus say about the incident in terms of its…*
- *motive?*
- *meaning?*
- *legacy?*

Read Matthew 26:14-16

❓ *How do Judas' actions contrast with the woman's?*

This is another theme we'll see repeated: Jesus is in total control of the action (see how verse 16 echoes verse 2), but people are also totally responsible for their actions.

Most of us can't help but speculate: *why did Judas do it?* Matthew doesn't really tell us. But in structuring the narrative this way, he does invite us to make a comparison between two different people with two different attitudes towards Jesus. One values him more highly than a treasured family heirloom; the other thinks he's worth no more than the price of a slave (see Exodus 21:32). One gives to him generously; the other sells him out short. One honours him in public; the other betrays him in secret.

We'll see Judas face the consequences later. But in Matthew 26:13 Jesus promises an extraordinary reward to the woman—and as you read these words of Jesus 2,000 years later, they continue to come true.

⌄ Apply

When you live your life making much of Jesus, he promises to one day make much of you (see also 25:34-35).

❓ *How does Jesus' control over the situation in Matthew 26 move you to value him highly, give to him generously and honour him publicly?*

❓ *What "beautiful thing" could you do for Jesus today? This week?*

Passover: this is…

There are more mealtime surprises in store for the disciples. It's Passover—a special annual festival to remember the Israelites' rescue from slavery in Egypt.

Who? Me?

Read Matthew 26:17-25

❓ *What surprising turn does this dinner take?*

❓ *In these verses, how do we see:*
- *Jesus' total control over the action?*
- *Judas' total responsibility for his own actions?*

The intimacy of this private dinner between friends is shattered with Jesus' declaration in verse 21—there is a traitor at the table. It's like having Christmas dinner with your nearest and dearest, only for the host to look around the table and declare that someone there is going to stab them in the back. No wonder the disciples are shocked and confused. Sometimes we would do well to mirror their self-examination: *I wouldn't do that to you, Jesus... would I?*

Verse 25 is outrageous. Judas, with the chief priest's 30 silver coins in his pocket, looks Jesus in the eye and feigns total innocence.

Body and blood

Read Matthew 26:26-30

❓ *What surprising turn does this dinner take now? Why would this have been shocking for the disciples?*

It is significant that Jesus says this at Passover (see Exodus 12).

❓ *What is he saying about Passover?*

❓ *What is he saying about himself?*

Jesus' words may be very familiar to us, but they were the opposite for the disciples. For centuries, this moment in the Passover had been marked with the words, "This is the bread of affliction which our fathers ate in the wilderness". Now, "This is my body".

❓ *What hope does Jesus offer to his shocked, confused disciples?*

Jesus is clear: his life won't be "taken" from him. He is willingly "giving" his body and blood on behalf of his friends. As painful as the next day will be, his death won't be a tragic waste. It will secure "forgiveness of sins", not just for these few followers in a room in Jerusalem, but "for many". His death will mean that every follower of Jesus can feast with him at heaven's banquet—a "new" meal with all the intimacy but none of the sadness of this supper.

⌄ Apply

While Jesus will not drink of the cup again until his people are with him in the kingdom of heaven, his followers do. "Whenever you eat this bread and drink this cup, you proclaim the Lord's death until he comes" (1 Corinthians 11:26).

❓ *What have you been struck by in this passage that you want to keep in mind next time you take the Lord's Supper at your church?*

He did not falter

With 30 silver coins in his pocket, Judas looked Jesus in the eye and lied. Now, sword at his side, another friend looks Jesus in the eye and makes a promise he can't keep…

Not as I will…
Read Matthew 26:31-44

❷ *What does Jesus say is going to happen, and why (v 31-32)?*
❷ *How do Peter and the other disciples respond (v 33-35)?*
❷ *When Jesus and the disciples arrive at Gethsemane, what does Jesus want from his friends? Why, do you think?*
❷ *Is Peter able to stand by Jesus in this hour of need? Why/why not (v 41, 43)?*

From eternity past, God's Son had existed in a relationship of perfect love with "his Father"—so the prospect of experiencing the cup of God's wrath on the cross over-whelmed him with unfathomable sorrow. He was desperate for there to be another way—but he was ready to submit to his Father's will if there wasn't one (v 39).

In many ways, Jesus' second prayer (v 42) is the most moving. He's just found his friends sleeping through his hour of need. *Fine, drink your own share of God's wrath,* we might respond. Yet Jesus, despite their weakness, is still prepared to "take away" the wrath they face by bearing it for them.

And unlike the disciples, he won't fail. His resolve to submit to his Father won't falter.

▲ Pray

If it was down to any other man on that hillside, we would still be facing God's wrath (a prospect so awful that it ought to make us tremble, as it did Jesus). But it wasn't down to any other man. It was down to Jesus. His spirit was willing, and he was far from weak.

❷ *What do you want to say to Jesus right now?*
❷ *"Yet not as I will, but as you will" (v 39). Is there an area of your life where you need to say that to God? Will you do that now, and ask him to help you to mean it?*

… but as you will
Read Matthew 26:45-56

❷ *What do you find particularly outrageous about Judas' betrayal (v 47-50)?*
❷ *What details of the betrayal does Matthew emphasise (v 47-50)?*
❷ *In what ways do we see Jesus…*
  • *in total control of the situation?*
  • *submitting to the Father's will, as he said that he would?*

Jesus' words in verse 31 come true with this short, tragic statement: "Then all the disciples deserted him and fled" (v 56).

▼ Apply

❷ *Might you be at risk of false confidence, like Peter? In what areas?*

Faithfulness and denial

Next, Matthew shows us two men facing questioning—and invites us to compare how they respond.

Faithful Jesus
Read Matthew 26:57-68

❷ *The chief priests are looking for a charge against Jesus—what accusation finally sticks? Is it true (see John 2:19-21)?*

❷ *Why does Jesus stay silent in Matthew 26:63, do you think (see Isaiah 53:7)?*

Caiaphas ups the ante in Matthew 26:63 by compelling Jesus to answer under oath: is he or isn't he the Messiah—the anointed king sent by God?

❷ *What do you make of Jesus' answer?*

····**TIME OUT**···
Read Psalm 110 and Daniel 7:13-14

❷ *What claim is Jesus making in Matthew 26:64?*

It looks as if Jesus is weak and Caiaphas holds all the cards. But not for much longer. The earthly high priest will cease to be that when Christ is made "priest for ever, in the order of Melchizedek" (Psalm 110:4). Although Caiaphas sits in the judgment seat now, one day the man in front of him "will judge nations" (v 6). So the temple as the centre of right worship has indeed been done away with (Matthew 26:61) through Jesus' death and resurrection.

Determined to secure the conviction, the high priest makes a show of tearing his robes and twice declares that Jesus' words are blasphemous. The council declares that Jesus is "worthy of death". But in rejecting God's Messiah, *they* are the ones who are committing blasphemy and are worthy of death. Each gobbet they spit into the face of God's Son only compounds their guilt.

In doing these things, they fulfil the very words that Jesus has previously spoken. They prove that he is indeed a true prophet even as they mock him for being false.

Faithless Peter
Read Matthew 26:69-75

❷ *How does this scene compare with the previous one in terms of...*
• who's asking the question?
• how Jesus/Peter responds?

Jesus stayed faithful under trial, declaring his identity as the Son of God even at the cost his life. Peter proves faithless under trial—he disowns Jesus to protect his life.

⌄ Apply

❷ *Have you ever "wept bitterly" over times when you've let Jesus down (v 75)? How is our faith impoverished if we never own and feel our sinfulness?*

❷ *What do you know of the rest of Peter's story that encourages you, even as you read of his denials here (see, for example, John 21)?*

Me, who caused his pain

It's now early Friday morning. Because the Jewish leaders don't have the authority to execute Jesus, they pass him on to the Roman authorities, who do.

But something else is being passed around too: the buck. It seems that no one wants to take responsibility for what is about to happen to Jesus...

Read Matthew 27:1-10

> ❷ *Who do we see trying to pass on responsibility for Jesus' death? Why?*
> ❷ *Who really is responsible, do you think?*
> ❷ *At the same time, who is ultimately in control of the action (v 9-10; compare also 27:1 and 26:1-2)?*

By putting this scene straight after 26:69-75, Matthew sets up an interesting comparison between Peter and Judas. Michael Green reflects: "Remorse is destructive, repentance is creative. So Judas went to destruction and Peter became a new man whom Christ could use and rely on" (*The Message of Matthew*, page 287).

Read Matthew 27:11-26

> ❷ *What similarities do you see between this trial before Pilate and the previous trial before the religious leaders (26:57-68)? Find as many as you can.*
> ❷ *Who is Jesus passed from, and to (v 26)? Why?*
> ❷ *Who do we see trying to pass on responsibility for Jesus' death? Why?*
> ❷ *Who really is responsible, do you think?*

Pilate is caught between the baying crowd, his insistent wife, the scheming religious leaders—and this curiously silent man, Jesus (v 14). It seems that Pilate thinks he's innocent (v 19, notice also v 4), but his plan to get him released as that year's choice of "bonus Passover prisoner release" backfires. Yet Pilate's show of handwashing will do nothing to absolve his part in this horrific episode of history.

Finally, it's the crowd who claims responsibility for Jesus' impending execution: "His blood is on us and on our children!" (v 25). They're the words of a worked-up mob making a show of defiance—but they have a chilling ring of truth to them. Jesus' blood is on every person of every generation who rejects him as King. **Read Acts 2:22-24, 36-39.**

To really grasp the wonder of Easter, we need to look at the cross and recognise our guilt. We need to say with tears in our eyes, "His blood is on me. It was my sin that did that." Then, wonderfully, "his blood is on me" becomes "my guilt is on him". Like guilty Barabbas, we can be set free—because the innocent Son of God silently submitted himself to judgment.

⌃ Pray

And can it be that I should gain
An int'rest in the Saviour's blood?
Died he for me, who caused his pain?
For me, who him to death pursued?
Amazing love! how can it be
That thou, my God, should die for me?

(Charles Wesley)

Surely he is...

In 24 hours Jesus has been betrayed by a friend, abandoned by his followers, framed by the religious leaders, and failed by the governor. Now it's the soldiers' turn...

Total fraud?

Try to really imagine all that Matthew is describing as you...

Read Matthew 27:27-50

❷ *Which detail shocks you most?*
❷ *What do you think the following people "see" when they look at Jesus?*
  • *The Roman soldiers (v 27-37)*
  • *The bystanders (v 39-40)*
  • *The religious leaders (v 41-43)*
  • *The rebels (v 38, 44)*
❷ *What does Matthew want us to "see" when we look at Jesus (v 29, 37, 42)?*

As Jesus hangs there, naked and bloodied, the people's taunts point us to the obvious conclusion: he's *not* the King of the Jews (v 37); he's *not* the Son of God (v 40); he *can't* save anyone (v 42); and God *doesn't* want this so-called Son (v 43). Even Jesus himself is distraught at his Father's rejection, crying out in agony: *Where are you, God?*

What is God's reply to this scene? A dark, chilling silence. He's not coming to Jesus' rescue; neither is Elijah (v 49). As Jesus dies, it seems that the scoffers are right. But here comes the twist...

Or Son of God?

Read Matthew 27:51-54

❷ *In verse 46, Jesus asked "Why?" What answers do these verses point to?*
  • *v 51*   • *v 52-53*

For hundreds of years, the temple curtain separated sinful people from God's presence in the Most Holy Place. But now "we have confidence to enter the Most Holy Place by the blood of Jesus, by a new and living way opened for us through the curtain, that is, his body" (Hebrews 10:19-20). Why was Jesus forsaken on the cross? To give us access to the Father and restore our relationship with him.

The curious incident in verses 52-53 is found only Matthew's Gospel, and leaves us with questions: When exactly did these resurrections happen? Is the "holy city" (v 53) the earthly Jerusalem, or perhaps the heavenly one? But the meaning Matthew is pointing us to is clearer...

Why was Jesus forsaken on the cross? To give us eternal life and the hope of a resurrection beyond the grave: "But Christ has indeed been raised from the dead, the firstfruits of those who have fallen asleep" (1 Corinthians 15:20).

Jesus was not a fraud: "Surely he was the Son of God!" He *is* the King; he *can* save us; and God *loves* his Son, and loves those who belong to his Son. And it's all because of the events of Good Friday.

⌃ Pray

❷ *What do you want to say to King Jesus now?*

Deity in the dust

Today is what is known in some church traditions as "Holy Saturday". Centuries of Christians have observed it as a time of waiting and reflection.

Borrowed tomb
Read Matthew 27:55-61

The Sabbath day (when no work was permitted) went from sunset on Friday to sunset on Saturday. Jewish law dictated that dead bodies should not be left overnight (Deuteronomy 21:22-23). It was normal for the Romans to throw the bodies of criminals like Jesus into a trench in a field.

❷ *How then would you describe Joseph's actions here? What is motivating him?*
❷ *What do you think these followers of Jesus are feeling... thinking... expecting?*
❷ *Why do you think Matthew mentions these women (Matthew 27:55-56, 61)?*

···· TIME OUT ·····················

Read Isaiah 53:7-11

❷ *Look at verse 9. Which part of Isaiah's prophecy do we see coming true in Matthew 27:57-61?*
❷ *What does Isaiah hint will come next?*

Sealed tomb
Read Matthew 27:62-66

❷ *What is hypocritical about what the chief priests and Pharisees are doing on the Sabbath (see 12:1-14)?*
❷ *What are the they concerned about? Why might Pilate share their concern?*
❷ *What precautions do they take as a result of their concerns?*

Jesus is dead and buried, so on the face of it the religious leaders' scheming has been a success. But they can't shake the feeling that this isn't the end of the matter. While they dismiss Jesus as a "deceiver", they're afraid enough of his power (or the power of his reputation) to come crawling to Pilate for help—even on the Sabbath.

In 27:65, it's not clear whether Pilate is telling them to use their own guards (from the temple) and is therefore rejecting their request, or if he's giving them Roman guards to use. Either way, the end result is a lock-stock-and-barrel shutting up of the tomb. Notice how the word "secure" is used three times in the space of three verses (v 64-66).

The religious leaders make the tomb "as secure as [they] know how"—but will it be secure enough? That's for tomorrow. Until then, we imagine ourselves with the disciples: watching, waiting, grieving. The author of life is dead and buried, having taken our place in the grave (v 60).

⌃ Pray

Low in the grave he lay, Jesus my Saviour,
Waiting the coming day, Jesus my Lord!
Vainly they watch his bed, Jesus my Saviour,
Vainly they seal the dead, Jesus my Lord!
Death cannot keep its prey, Jesus my Saviour;
He tore the bars away, Jesus my Lord!

(Robert Lowry)

Up from the grave!

HAPPY RESURRECTION SUNDAY! Late on Friday afternoon, the women had watched as their friend was laid in the tomb. Now, a little over 36 hours later, they return…

He is risen!
Read Matthew 28:1-10

On a scale of 1-10, the religious leaders' security measures from yesterday score zero. The angel makes it look so easy!

> ❷ *Why does the angel open the tomb, do you think (v 6)? What's his take-home message (or rather, his take-to-the-disciples message)?*

Chart the emotional journey that the women go on through these verses.

> ❷ *Why are they afraid? Why are they told to "not be afraid" (v 5, 10)?*

Mary and Mary have experienced an earthquake, encountered a fearsome supernatural being, and been given a piece of news no grieving person expects to hear: *Your friend was dead, but they're not dead anymore.*

As they rush away from the tomb, with their hearts beating and the adrenaline pumping—Jesus appears! And says, in effect… *Hi!* It's personal and familiar. But the women's response to the risen Jesus is far from casual—they fall at his feet and worship him as God.

⌄ Apply

Jesus is risen—and he is King! He has so much life and power that nothing and no one can hold him down. He cannot be foiled. He has total authority over death.

What he says will happen, happens. He is, in the true sense of the word, *awesome.*

> ❷ *In what area of your life do you particularly need to remember that?*

Jesus is risen—and he is your brother (v 10)! Your relationship is personal and familiar. He greets you with tenderness and love. He doesn't want you to feel afraid.

> ❷ *In what area of your life do you particularly need to remember that?*

Yes, really
Read Matthew 28:11-15

> ❷ *What plan do the leaders cook up now?*
> ❷ *What are some of the holes in the guards' story (v 13)?*

⌄ Apply

> ❷ *How would you use these verses to help persuade a non-Christian friend that the resurrection really happened?*
> ❷ *What else would you want to say about why that's such exciting news?*

⌃ Pray

"They came to him, clasped his feet and worshipped him" (v 9). Jesus is alive right now, listening to you! Come to him; worship him as King; speak to him as your brother. Perhaps listen to or sing a favourite Easter hymn.

Bible in a year: Daniel 8-10 • Revelation 8 ✔

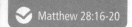
All about him

The women were sent from the tomb with a message for the disciples: "[Jesus] has risen from the dead and is going ahead of you into Galilee. There you will see him" (v 7).

Of all the things Jesus could say to the disciples, what will he say?

Go therefore…

Read Matthew 28:16-20

- ❷ *How do the disciples respond when they see Jesus?*
- ❷ *"But some doubted" (v 17). Does that surprise you? Why/why not?*
- ❷ *Why has Jesus been given "all authority" by the Father (v 18)? What has happened in the last three chapters which shows that is true?*
- ❷ *What are the disciples called to do as a consequence of Jesus having all authority (v 19-20)? What's the link?*
- ❷ *What reassurance are the disciples given in the face of this mammoth task (v 20)?*

···· TIME OUT ·····························

Read Matthew 26:31-32

- ❷ *When were the disciples "scattered" the first time?*
- ❷ *Having been "gathered" in Galilee, in what way are they being "scattered" again in 28:18-20?*
- ❷ *What are some of the big differences this time round?*

⌄ Apply

So often when these verses are wheeled out, we're left feeling guilty and inadequate about our evangelism. But in some ways, that takes us closer to the mood in chapter 28. The disciples' "doubt" in verse 17 suggests some fear and trepidation at least. After all, these are the same men who "all … deserted [Jesus] and fled" in 26:56.

Yet none of that stops Jesus from entrusting them with this most important of missions. Their doubts and previous failures don't matter, because they're being sent not on their own authority but on his—and he has all authority. The same is true for us today.

And as you sit reading *Explore* 2,000 years later, you are living proof that Jesus' promise to his first disciples held true as they obeyed this commission. And it still holds true today. You are one of many, many people from many, many nations that the gospel has reached—Jesus is unstoppable!

⌃ Pray

All authority: Worship Jesus—the risen King, who is reigning today.

All nations: Pray for a people group far away, and for people you know closer to home.

Everything: Pray that you would faithfully communicate the whole truth of Jesus' words to others, not ducking out of the difficult parts.

Always: Praise Jesus that he is with you; ask him to help you to remember that next time you're called to take a risk to proclaim who he is and why he came.

ACTS: Guilty of what?

Paul has appeared before the Sanhedrin. Now he must appear before the Roman governor. He is, in one sense, following in the footsteps of the Lord Jesus.

Case for the prosecution

Read Acts 24:1-9

Ananias is a complicated figure. He was appointed high priest in AD 47 and known for having an explosive temper. He was deposed by King Agrippa in AD 59 and murdered by Jewish assassins six years later. The fact that he shows up to prosecute the case against Paul sends a serious signal. It would be the equivalent of the President of the United States showing up to prosecute a trial taking place in the Supreme Court.

❷ *Why does Ananias' lawyer, Tertullus, start his speech in the way he does, do you think (v 2-4)?*

❷ *What does he accuse Paul of (v 5-6)?*

❷ *To what extent is Paul guilty of these charges?*

Case for the defence

Read Acts 24:10-21

Paul's opening lines to Felix are in stark contrast to Tertullus' greeting. Rather than resort to flattery, Paul simply states the facts about Felix's rule. He stands confidently on the solid ground of the gospel, which is why he can make his defence cheerfully and with integrity.

❷ *How does Paul seek to answer the accusations levelled against him (v 11-13, 17-18)?*

❷ *What is the one "charge" which he cheerfully agrees he is guilty of (v 14-15, 21)?*

As Paul concludes his defence in verses 18–21, he seizes the opportunity not only to assert his innocence but also to declare his hope in the resurrection of the dead. Paul's words before the Sanhedrin and his words here before Felix point to the theological issue at the heart of his disagreement with Ananias. Paul recognises that this conflict has nothing to do with Rome and its peace; it has everything to do with those who believe the gospel and those who reject it.

✔ Apply

Paul was able with integrity to say he was innocent of wrongdoing, and was guilty only of being a "follower of the Way", who believed in "the resurrection of the dead" (v 14, 21). The question this poses for us is:, to what extent could we say this?

❷ *Are there areas of your life where a charge of ungodliness, or breaking the law of your land, could stick?*

Don't make excuses. Repent, and change.

❷ *And if someone looked at your life, would they find you guilty of being a "follower of the Way", who lives as though "the resurrection of the dead" is a future reality? Why/why not?*

Listening ≠ repenting

The prosecution and defence have made their cases. Now it is time for... no verdict.

The adjournment
Read Acts 24:22-23

It seems Felix has realised that Ananias is armed only with baseless accusation. From this point, the Jews have nothing on Paul. His case becomes a matter of the Roman judicial process—exactly as God intended.

The discussions
Read Acts 24:24

❓ *How would you describe Felix's spiritual state (v 22, 24)?*

It was not surprising that the governor knew something of the Christian faith, since the gospel had taken root in Caesarea decades before (10:44–46).

Here we are also introduced to Drusilla, Felix's wife—who had left her previous husband to marry him.

Read Acts 24:25-27

❓ *Why would the aspects of God's revelation that Luke mentions in verse 25 have made Felix "afraid"?*
❓ *How does he respond to hearing these truths (v 25)?*

Acts presents its reader with spectacular stories of conversions and repentance—not least, of Paul himself. But at the same time, the Scriptures present a real and unembellished story. Paul's message of righteousness and self-control challenged Felix and Drusilla because they were entrenched in sin and disobedience. Preaching the gospel means preaching conversion, repentance, and a turning away from sin. Responding to the gospel means recognising Christ to be Lord over our desires and relationships. Felix's refusal to do more than listen is a sobering reminder that listening, however regular and interested it may be, is not sufficient—repentance is necessary.

❓ *When Felix faces the choice between doing what is right and doing what is popular, what does he choose (v 27)?*

▼ Apply

You may be reading this page having listened to God's word with interest, regularly, for months or years...

❓ *Will you now repent, accept Jesus as your Lord, and find forgiveness before you face his judgment?*

You may be reading this page knowing that there are times when you choose popularity (or at least you won't risk unpopularity) ahead of doing what is right for the sake of the gospel; or when, unlike Paul, you do not warn others of the judgment to come...

❓ *Will you now repent of that, and ask Jesus to be your Lord next time you must choose between doing what is right and what is popular, or between speaking what is true and what is popular?*

Jerusalem or Rome?

In Acts 25, Luke never mentions the name of God. The hand of God, however, is at work throughout the entire narrative. God orchestrates every event in this chapter.

The Jews try again

Read Acts 25:1-7

Festus is the new governor (24:27), and he comes from a very different background than Felix. Festus was a blue-blood Roman whose family had long been influential in the empire. Felix, it seems, had left things in such a mess that Rome was determined to send someone of noble pedigree to try to clean up the mess that was made in Judea.

❷ *What do the Jews want, and what does Festus give them (25:3, 4-5)?*

Festus strikes an authoritative balance. On the one hand, he assuages the Jews by continuing the legal proceedings against Paul. On the other, by setting the location of the trial in Caesarea, he reminds the Jews of his power as the Roman governor.

❷ *What is the problem for the Jewish leaders (v 7)?*

I appeal to Caesar!

Read Acts 25:8-12

Paul's defence in v 8 suggests that the Jews indicted Paul on charges involving each of those three institutions. The Jewish leaders wanted him executed. They knew they would have to charge Paul with more than teaching erroneous doctrines. They needed to make him out to be a seditious charlatan. So they adopted a strategy similar to the one they had employed against Jesus. When the

King of kings had stood in their presence, the leaders of the Jewish people—the promised people of God—had exclaimed, "We have no king but Caesar" (John 19:15)!

❷ *How does Festus seek to appease the Jews (Acts 25:9)?*

Festus shows his true colours. He concerns himself with regional stability, not justice.

❷ *What would the consequence of going to Jerusalem be for Paul (v 3)?*
❷ *How does Paul respond, and with what result (v 10-12)?*

This was the right of every Roman citizen. And the reader knows, of course, that this was also the sovereign plan of God (23:11). The coming narrative will demonstrate that Paul's situation in no way surprised God or caught God off guard—quite the reverse.

⌄ Apply

Today, Christians will meet opposition and persecution, and face accusations. Western Christians will stand trial in the cultural courts of modernity. The high priests of the moral revolution will charge Christians with sedition. They will indict Christians for holding antiquated beliefs which oppose the new post-Christian status quo. Indeed, Western culture continues to view Christian dogma as diametrically opposed to progress. The question, therefore, is this: *are God's people willing to continue to live out and speak out the gospel truth?*

Making Jesus the issue

Paul's lifetime of faithfulness and God's gracious hand now bring Paul to a crucial moment in his ministry. He will proclaim the gospel before a king.

Two Roman rulers
Read Acts 25:13-22

King Agrippa and his sister Bernice had one of the most infamous incestuous relationships in ancient history. Emperor Claudius had ordered Bernice to marry (someone other than her brother, obviously), but she almost immediately left her marriage to go back and live as her brother's consort.

Festus wants to discuss Paul's case with this local king installed by Rome who is more knowledgeable about local culture and religion than the governor.

> ❷ *What has perplexed Festus (v 18-19)?*
> ❷ *What help does Agrippa seem to be able to give (v 22)?!*

Do not miss what happens here: two *Roman rulers* discuss the resurrection of Jesus!

☑ Apply

Acts 25 reveals a conversation between two secular rulers who have started discussing the gospel because of Paul's witness. When we share the gospel, we hope to see a person repent and believe on the spot. Rarely do such conversions happen. When someone comes to faith, there has probably been a long line of faithful witnesses who have shared Christ with them. When you share the gospel, you cast a seed which may germinate and take root later on. You do not know how God will use your faithfulness.

> ❷ *How does this encourage you today? In whom might you seek to plant a seed?*

An elite congregation
Read Acts 25:23-27

> ❷ *Who gathers to hear from Paul (v 23)?*

Do you see what God did here? An elite, unsuspecting congregation were drawn together who must have believed they held the power and authority. Then a man in chains appeared before them—and it was that man who was truly free and who alone knew what could set the entire room free— not from Roman law but from God's wrath.

> ❷ *How does Festus compare the Jews and the apostle (v 24-25)?*

☑ Apply

In the same way, the world watches Christians and their actions. Our conduct can bear tremendous fruit among non-believers or harm the witness of the gospel. Hypocrisy kills the credibility of any Christian. Paul not only needed to believe the truth but to live it, in order to gain a hearing for that truth. Do we? **Read 1 Peter 2:12.**

> ❷ *How does this encourage you? Are there "charges" that would stick against you? If so, to whom do you need to apologise and in what ways do you need to change your conduct?*

Giving up goad-kicking

Writing letters in the ancient world was expensive. Every word bore a cost. So for Luke to record Paul's speech in full here means he viewed it as a significant moment.

Before Damascus

Read Acts 26:1-11

❓ *What does Paul say about:*
- *his religious views prior to his trip to Damascus (v 4-5)?*
- *the relationship between what he used to believe and what he now believes (v 6-8)?*
- *his view of Christianity prior to that famous journey to Damascus (v 9-11)?*

Do not underestimate the power of personal narrative in sharing the gospel. Telling others of God's saving work in our lives connects nonbelievers to the gospel in a powerful way. Sharing your testimony will not only communicate the truth of Christ but show how his grace worked on you.

Paul is building anticipation in his audience. How could this man, once a persecutor of Christians and agent of the Jewish elite, now stand condemned by those very authorities? What had happened in Paul's life to radically alter his course?

After Damascus

Read Acts 26:12-16

Jesus' phrase "It is hard for you to kick against the goads" (v 14) reveals he'd been at work in Paul's life for a long time. Jesus had been prodding Paul towards himself throughout his life. Paul, however, "kicked against the goads": a phrase meaning he, in futility, attempted to resist the power of Jesus Christ. Paul resisted, but God pursued.

❓ *What does Jesus' reply to Paul's question in verse 15 remind us about the Lord's relationship to his church?*
❓ *What was the purpose of Jesus revealing himself to Paul (v 16)?*

⌄ Apply

If God's will beats the drum of your life and led you to that moment of saving faith, then every moment of your life bears an eternal significance. Suffering, trials, pain, darkness, depression, sickness, and a life engrossed in the vilest of sin have all shaped and become gospel gems in your testimony.

❓ *How should that change the way you think and speak about your past?*

⌃ Pray

Paul's testimony should influence our prayers. As believers, we can and should pray for our non-believing family members and friends—that the goads would be too sharp and prove too exhausting to continue to resist. We can pray that God would use life's circumstances to show people their need for Jesus Christ.

Pray now for whoever the Lord is placing on your heart. Ask him to make them weary of kicking against the goads, and to reveal himself to them.

Cash values

Proverbs has a lot to say about work and our attitude towards money, wealth and poverty. Here's a clutch of sayings that sum up its general themes in this area.

We tend to think that money and work are things that are only important for this life—and that "spiritual" things are about the next. How wrong could we be?

Read Proverbs 10:2-5

- ❓ *What is at stake in our attitude to money (v 2)?*
- ❓ *Why do you think treasures and righteousness are compared with each other?*
- ❓ *What is promised (v 3)?*
- ❓ *What general principle is laid out in verse 4?*
- ❓ *How have you seen that in your life, and in the lives of others?*
- ❓ *What is being encouraged in verse 5?*
- ❓ *Can you think of a modern, non-agricultural version of this proverb?*

Wisdom is, quite literally, a matter of life and death. It might seem strange to juxtapose ill-gotten treasures with righteousness, but that is one of the brilliant things about these proverbs. On the surface, they can seem simple; but beneath it, there are some profound things going on. It's true, of course, that in general someone who steals, cheats or swindles their way to riches is in a precarious position with regard to the law—and it's true that no one can take their riches with them into the next world. But it runs deeper than that. Only righteousness can deliver us from the ultimate enemy—death. And that righteousness is only available to us as a gift from God in the gospel of Christ.

Yeah, but…

Read Proverbs 10:3-4 again

- ❓ *Can you think of instances where these proverbs are not true?*
- ❓ *Does that confuse you?*

Proverbs often come in pairs. Too many cooks spoil the broth. Many hands make light work. It might seem that this makes them wrong, or contradictory—but not so. Many proverbs are designed to work in *specific situations*, not in the abstract. We might know of instances where the righteous have starved; or where lazy people have got rich and hard-working diligent people have remained poor. But these are instances against the run of normal life. They are exceptions that prove the rule, we might say. We mustn't forget that underlying all that Proverbs says is the knowledge that God is at work in the world. These are not *inevitable* principles of life. Life is usually like this because God chooses to bless those who are careful workers like himself, and to judge (if not in this world, then in the next) those who try to "game" life to their advantage.

⌃ Pray

Pray that you would please God in how you work and live this coming week.

You need what I have

Jesus has informed Paul that he will now live as a servant of Christ, not a persecutor of Christ. Next, Paul recounts what that servanthood was to look like for him.

Read Acts 26:16-20

❓ *To whom was Paul being sent (v 17-18)?*
❓ *In what three ways does Jesus describe what the effects of Paul's witness will be (v 18)?*
❓ *How did Paul respond to Jesus' words (v 19)?*

There is no such thing as a neutral answer to God's revelation. We will either respond in obedience or rejection. Paul obeyed. He declared his faith to those in Damascus and then progressively throughout the region and then to the Gentile world (v 20).

❓ *What did his preaching urge both Jews and Gentiles to do (v 20)?*

This phrase balances the two gospel themes of grace and good works. We are saved by repenting, but coming under the lordship of Jesus will always show itself in deeds done in obedience to him.

The governor's response

Read Acts 26:21-26

❓ *When Paul mentions Jesus' resurrection (v 23), what does Festus do (v 24)?*
❓ *How does Paul answer him (v 25-26)?*

The Christian gospel is not irrational. On the other hand, the gospel is not rationalistic. None come to understand the gospel through an intellectual exercise or display of superior powers of reason. We do not figure out the gospel through our own ingenuity.

The gospel is rational, but minds darkened by sin cannot grasp its assertions—as Festus here shows.

The king's response

Read Acts 26:27-30

❓ *How does Paul seek to challenge Agrippa, and how does Agrippa seek to deflect the challenge (v 27-28)?*

Paul responds to Agrippa's question with an appeal to the entire audience. He, a prisoner in chains, says to the king in his royal robes and the crowds of cultural elites, *However high you climb and whatever wealth you enjoy, you do not have what I have found. You ache for what I possess, and you need it far more than you realise.* The eternal riches of Christ eclipse all the wealth this world can offer.

☑ Apply

This is why we preach the gospel—that others might enjoy the splendour and majesty of Christ. How can we keep it to ourselves?

❓ *Do you know an Agrippa—someone who is doing well in this life—and so you forget that they most need riches in eternal life? How will you pray for them? How will you seek to share the gospel with them?*
❓ *Do you know a Festus—someone who thinks the resurrection is irrational? How will you pray for them? How will you seek to persuade them otherwise?*

Bible in a year: Numbers 5-6 • Revelation 16 ✔

Courage in the storm

Remember, Paul knows where he is heading, because Jesus has said, "As you have testified about me in Jerusalem, so you must also testify in Rome" (23:11).

The plan continues

Read Acts 26:30-32

Paul could have been released if he had not appealed to Caesar. But he had—so Agrippa had no choice but to send Paul to Rome. That was exactly what Paul wanted, and precisely what God intended.

From bad to worse

Read Acts 27:1-20

The Jews feared the sea, possibly due to the Old Testament accounts of Noah and Jonah. Paul was probably nervous as he boarded (v 2). The journey's timing also speaks ominously. The best seasons for navigating the Mediterranean are spring and summer. This trip took place after the Day of Atonement in mid-October (v 9).

❷ *How do things go on the journey?*
- *verses 3-5*   • *verses 6-8*
- *verses 12-13*   • *verses 14-17*
- *verses 18-20*

Trusting God's promise

Read Acts 27:21-26

❷ *What does Paul urge the crew and passengers to do, and why (v 22)?*
❷ *Why is he so confident of this (v 23-24)?*

Notice three things:

1. *Paul exudes an unyielding confidence in God's sovereign will.* He never allows his cir-

cumstances to dictate his theology. We can jettison our hope in God's will when heavy traffic threatens to make us late for an appointment. Paul maintained his confidence in God when shipwreck looked certain!

2. *Paul remains confident even when his current circumstances seem unnecessary.* If God intended Paul to testify to the gospel before Caesar, why then did Paul have to endure more trials and more difficulty? Acts 27 reveals that the road might be longer and harder than we imagined—but that God will have his reasons for that. Here, Paul is able to witness to the ship's crew *because* of their perilous situation.

3. *Though Paul rests in God's sovereign hand, he knows that people still need to act.* They "must run aground" (v 26) and then they will have to swim to shore. Paul calls the ship to faith in God, while also directing them to run the ship aground as an act of faith. While we must trust in God's will and his sovereign purposes, our trust evidences itself through acts of obedience.

◢ Apply

❷ *Are you facing a trial—a diversion from your own plans for your life?*
❷ *Will you trust in the truths Paul did?*

God has *not* promised that you will stand trial before Caesar in Rome. God *has* promised that you will stand in joy before God in heaven!

Will God come through?

Paul is still a prisoner on his way to trial. But he is now also effectively in charge of the ship. So the question is: will his confidence in God's promise prove well-founded?

Making their decision
Read Acts 27:27-32

❓ Why do the sailors lower the lifeboat (v 28-30)?

❓ How do they respond to Paul's warning (v 32)?

Paul does not offer sound nautical counsel because the issue here is not one of nautical science, but theology. Will the sailors trust in their own plans or in those of Paul's God? In verse 32, they make their decision.

Making preparations
Read Acts 27:33-37

❓ How do these verses shows us Paul's calm trust in the providence of God?

No doubt Paul's conduct before the crew was an impactful gospel witness to them.

Making it to shore
Read Acts 27:38-44

Once the ship had struck a reef in open water, the front of the vessel was jammed but the back of the boat continued to be tossed by the sea (v 41). Naturally, the boat began to break apart.

The soldiers knew that if they went back to Rome without their prisoners, they would face the same judgment as the prisoners.

❓ What did they plan, and what stopped them (v 42-43)?

❓ Re-read v 23-26. To what extent did Paul's promise come true (v 43-44)?

❓ Imagine you had been a soldier or a sailor on that boat. What impression of Paul's God would you have been left with, as you reached land safely?

The whole chapter, right up to the very last verse, presents us with a remarkable picture of God's sovereignty and power. Nothing will thwart the will of God.

⌄ Apply

Paul endured much for the cause of the gospel. Paul pressed on because of God's promise. We fail in zealous obedience when we lose sight of the spectacular reward that awaits us. God has promised an eternity unlike anything we can imagine. He has promised that we will be with him, face to face, that death will be no more and sin will pass away. God calls his people to seize his promises and hold them tight. Our obedience will only be as strong as our faith in the promises of God. Paul told the 275 people on board with him to "take heart ... for I have faith in God that it will be exactly as I have been told" (v 25, ESV).

❓ In what ways do you need to take heart, trust in God's promises, and step out in faith-filled, risk-taking obedience?
❓ Will you actually do so today?

Neither killer nor God

Chapter 28 serves as a wonderful climactic end to this account of the Lord's work in the early church and its great expansion through the faithful witness of his servants.

The *karma* mistake

Read Acts 28:1-4

Once on land on the Mediterranean island of Malta, the travellers encountered islanders who showed all those from the ship extraordinary kindness, providing them with comfort and hospitality (v 2). Yet the narrative almost instantly confronts us with another remarkably unfortunate event in Paul's life.

❓ *What happens to him (v 3)?*

In a day when there was no antivenom, this certainly would lead to his death.

❓ *What do the islanders therefore conclude (v 4)?*

In the pagan worldview, the universe had judged Paul and struck him through the fangs of a venomous snake. This "cause-and-effect" worldview still exists in much of the world still today, and flows from notions like *karma*—you do something wrong in this universe, and the universe will repay you. So, the Maltese thinking went, a snake bit Paul because he had sinned. And now he would die.

The divinity mistake

Read Acts 28:5-6

❓ *What actually happens to Paul (v 5-6)?*
❓ *What do the islanders therefore conclude now (v 6)?*

Their view of the apostle moves from one extreme to the other. The islanders' worldview simply had no room for a gospel framework, in which a personal, powerful God works through people to show his goodness to his people and preach his truth to his world.

Read Acts 28:7-10

❓ *What does God do through Paul for Publius and many other islanders?*

Luke does not provide much information about the miracles in Malta. In other passages where crowds believed Paul was a god, Luke tells us exactly how Paul handled the situation and redirected such responses towards the gospel (see Acts 14:11-17). Here, Luke includes no such details—but we can be confident that if at any point Paul had begun to dignify the islanders' belief in his divinity, God would have removed his hand from Paul and his ministry. The presence of God with Paul on Malta, therefore, points to the gospel and power of God at work among the islanders and the shipwrecked crew.

☑ Apply

❓ *What kinds of phrases do you hear people say that fit with a "karma"-type view of how the world works?*
❓ *Do you ever look at the world in that way? How is the gospel a better message to sinners?*

And so to Rome

In today's passage, Paul finally reaches Rome—a journey that has taken him through various prisons, multiple trials, shipwreck and snakebite. God has proved faithful.

Read Acts 28:11-16

Finding the church

Puteoli (v 13) was a harbour near Naples, on the Italian mainland south of Rome.

❓ *What did Paul, Luke and the rest of Paul's companions discover in Puteoli (v 14)?*

❓ *How did they respond to Paul (v 14)?*

How did Christianity make it to Puteoli? We do not know, but this is a good reminder that the advancement of the gospel did not rest upon the shoulders of Paul alone. The hero of Acts is not Paul or Peter. It is God himself, who powerfully advanced the gospel throughout the known world, and by no means all of the details are recounted in the book of Acts. God has more zeal for kingdom work than any of the great missionaries in Christian history.

✅ Apply

God did not need Paul. He does not need you. He does, however, invite all his people to join in the mission of salvation.

❓ *How does this make you feel? How does it motivate you towards evangelism?*

Finding encouragement

"We came to Rome" (v 15)—the moment the narrative has been building to from 23:11.

❓ *Who has heard that Paul is coming, and how do they respond (28:15)?*

❓ *What impact does this have on Paul (v 15)?*

Even the apostle Paul needed encouragement. He faced an enormous trial—he would soon would have a face-to-face meeting with the most powerful man in the world, the emperor of the Roman Empire. Paul needed help, and he found it in the presence and welcome of God's people.

✅ Apply

Christian leaders today are often placed on pedestals—but they are (and can only be) ordinary people with hopes, fears and weaknesses. If you are in ministry leadership, never forget you need the help of those you serve.

❓ *Do you have good fellowship and accountability? How do you ensure that your own life remains accountable to other brothers and sisters in the faith?*

As a church member, never forget that a word of encouragement can go a long way in helping your leaders press on in faithful obedience. Like Paul, they may face significant challenges. They need you to encourage them without idolising them or flattering them.

❓ *How could you do this today?*

Where will *you* go?

When Paul arrives in Rome, we might expect him to go and get a good attorney. But defending himself is not his primary aim...

Read Acts 28:17-31

❓ *Who does Paul meet with (v 17)?*
❓ *What does he tell them about his situation (v 17-20)?*

Throughout Paul's ministry, the first place he went to in new cities was the synagogue. Paul cannot go to the synagogue in Rome, though, because he remains under house arrest. He therefore does the next best thing by inviting the Jewish leaders to his house.

❓ *What does Paul seek to persuade them of, and how, and with what results (v 23-25a)?*

Paul proclaimed to the Jews a prophetic word from Isaiah: God had spoken to Isaiah, indicating that even after Isaiah had preached, the people would not listen. God told Isaiah that his preaching would have no effect on the people of Israel. The people had hardened their hearts, shut their eyes, and turned away from God. In quoting from Isaiah 6, Paul applied this prophetic judgment to the Jews, who were placing themselves in a long line of hardened sinners who have rejected the promise of salvation secured through the Messiah.

❓ *So what would Paul do instead, and what was he confident of (Acts 28:28)?*
❓ *How would Paul's experience in his ministry throughout Acts have given him good grounds for such confidence?*
❓ *How are verses 30-31 a fitting end to this wonderful book?*

Luke's conclusion leaves us exactly where the Holy Spirit wants us—ready for the next chapter. That chapter continues to be written: the gospel still advances to the ends of the earth and God has called all his people to be part of it. Luke ends with an implied question: Peter preached the kingdom in Jerusalem; Philip proclaimed Christ in Samaria, Paul announced Christ around the Roman Empire... Where will you go?

We face a task unfinished—may God grant us the strength and courage to stand in that long line of Spirit-empowered, faithful witnesses which stretches all the way back to that unlikely band of first-century heroes.

⌄ Apply

❓ *Where will you go, and to whom will you proactively seek to speak about Jesus?*
❓ *How has the book of Acts:*
- *changed your priorities?*
- *changed your prayers?*
- *changed your view of God's mission and your place in it?*

⌃ Pray

Speak to God about your answers to the previous two questions. Commit yourself to witness in the power of his Spirit, for the glory of his Son, in whatever way he leads you.

Bible in a year: Numbers 17-19 • Revelation 21

Warning signs

Proverbs can urge us towards godly living, pass judgment on our failings, or, as in many of today's verses, offer us warnings to heed...

Words of warning
Read Proverbs 10:6-10

❓ *What general principle is outlined in verse 6?*
❓ *Why does verse 6 use the word "mouth", do you think (v 6)?*
❓ *What specific warnings are we given in each of verses 7-10?*
❓ *What is the common theme in verses 6-8 and verse 10?*

We may be tempted to apply the message of these proverbs to other people, but they are written for us too.

❓ *Which of these proverbs do you think you particularly need to heed today?*

I like to think of individual proverbs as being a bit like guided missiles. We might read through a chapter of these pithy sayings and nod in agreement with each of them, but then there is one that seems totally appropriate for us at the moment: an encouragement to keep going; a warning about something we are tempted towards; or a rebuke for some bit of ungodly thinking or behaviour we have got enmeshed in.

Our words, language and speech are another major theme in the book of Proverbs. It's not limited just to obvious issues such as lying or cussing. Verse 10 puts a secret gesture of contempt under the spotlight, as well as unguarded verbal diarrhoea. It is intriguing that verse 8 contrasts a chattering

fool with the "wise in heart [who] accept commands". The connection between our outward conduct and our hearts is never far from the surface in Scripture. In fact, our speech and attitudes *reveal* what is in our hearts.

🔼 Pray
Read Mark 7:21-23 and James 3:11-13

Talk to the Lord about your response to these verses.

Words of hope
Read Proverbs 10:7, 11-12

❓ *What positive visions for our speech and lives is presented in verses 11-12?*
❓ *What do you think it means that "love covers over all wrongs"?*
❓ *What will result from living like this (v 7)?*

To cover something is not to hide it but to forgive it. This verse ultimately points us towards Jesus and his work on the cross.

🔼 Pray

Pray that the first line of verse 11 would be true of you.

Ask God to pour his love for others into your heart, so that you would forgive others as Christ forgave you.

REVELATION: The end

We rejoin Revelation at the end. The end of the book. The end of the Bible. The end of history. John reveals the final spectacular visions given to him for our encouragement.

John is writing to Christians who are both tempted to join in with their alluring culture—and so compromise their faith—and who are suffering under direct persecution from the state—Rome. The whole aim of Revelation is to encourage Christians to remain faithful, whether they are facing temptation or martyrdom.

Part of the way Revelation does this is to remind us that earthly kingdoms are doomed, whereas the kingdom of Christ grows and reigns for ever.

Read Revelation 18:1-3

❓ *What is impressive about the description of the angel (messenger) in verse 1?*
❓ *Flick back over chapter 17. Who or what is "Babylon" that has fallen (18:2)?*
❓ *How complete is the fall of this once-great city (v 2)?*
❓ *Who else is implicated in the sins of Babylon (v 3)?*

Even though Rome is singled out, all nations are implicated in its destruction. It is the same today—all national economies are intertwined. A fall in the stock market in Tokyo can have dramatic effects around the rest of the world.

Read Revelation 18:4-8

❓ *What does the voice from heaven urge Christians to do and why (v 4)?*
❓ *What might this mean in practice?*
❓ *Who is ultimately responsible for the fall of Rome (v 5-6, 8)?*

❓ *What makes the judgment on Rome so fair (v 7)?*
❓ *What's the big difference between her sins and the judgment that comes to her (v 7-8)?*

We discover that the fall of Rome will be an act of divine judgment on her economic injustice and exploitation. Her judgment is just—that's the message of verses 4-8. The word "double" in verse 6 is better translated "duplicate". Her judgment duplicates her crimes. It is utterly and scrupulously fair.

⌄ Apply

"Come out of her" (v 4). John is not suggesting these Christians go into exile or create a ghetto in the hills. Elsewhere he calls for suffering witness in the midst of Rome. No, instead he wants us to adopt a different set of values, a different set of priorities, a different allegiance, a different object of worship. We move from citizenship on earth to citizenship in heaven. We pack our bags, leave our home in Babylon the Prostitute and set out for a new home in Jerusalem the Bride.

❓ *Where is this most challenging in your own life? What will it look like?*

⌃ Pray

Ask God to help you live out your true citizenship today in all that you do.

As Rome burns

The popular myth is that Nero fiddled as Rome burned. But here we see how the onlookers react to the downfall of the great empire.

In today's passage we see three groups of people who had earned their living from Rome, and their reaction to the judgment that has fallen upon her.

Kings of the earth
Read Revelation 18:9-10

❷ *What was the relationship of the kings of the earth to Rome (v 9)?*
❷ *Why do they weep and wail over her destruction?*
❷ *What are they afraid of (v 10)?*
❷ *What does this show about their relationship with God?*

There is no sign of any remorse among these kings. Rome had vanquished them, yes, but had also given them all the advantages of being citizens. They had lived in luxury. In some ways they seem to acknowledge the judgment is just, and yet they are only fearful that the torment should come to them. It does not lead them to repentance.

Merchants of the earth
Read Revelation 18:11-17a

❷ *What do the merchants weep over?*
❷ *What is the twist in the tale of the list in verses 12-13?*
❷ *What was it that the soul of Rome longed for (v 14)?*
❷ *Is there any remorse among the merchants?*

Seafaring men
Read Revelation 18:17b-20

❷ *What do the sailors seem to understand that the others miss (v 20)?*
❷ *Is their repentance genuine, do you think?*

All three groups "stand far off" (v 10, 15, 17). All three have enriched themselves from Rome. The sailors throw dust on their heads (v 19), and recognise that it is God's judgment upon them, but there is little sign that they embrace the alternative path. They have not "come out of her" (v 4).

⌄ Apply

The Lord Jesus taught that catastrophes are one way that God calls upon us to repent and turn to him (see Luke 13:1-5).

❷ *How should this shape your own responses to what you see on the news (or in your own life)?*
❷ *How will it shape the way you speak to others about such catastrophes?*

⌃ Pray

Pray for those you know who work in politics and business who are Christians. Ask God to help them know the true value of what they are doing. Pray for those who are working to bring the gospel message to those in politics and business.

Angel song

Above the wailing laments of the kings, merchants and seafarers, a different tune suddenly swells into life: not mourning the loss of the great city at all, but rejoicing...

Read Revelation 18:21-24

❓ *What is the symbolic significance of what the angel does in verse 21 (see Mark 9:42)?*

❓ *What is different about the angel's lament to those earlier in Revelation 18?*

❓ *Why does the angel rejoice that Rome has fallen silent, and that all economic life has ceased?*

❓ *What most incensed heaven about the behaviour of Rome (v 24)?*

John records the lament of those who have been blessed by Roman trade: the ruling elites (v 9-10), "the merchants" (v 11-17) and "the sailors" (v 17-20). It seems that he's inviting his readers to mourn with them over the collapse of the glories of Rome. But, as he does so, John sets a trap: those who lament the fall of Rome reveal the extent of their compromise. The image of a prostitute captures the way the world's economic system appears alluring while its underlying reality is ugly. If we find it hard to view our own society in this way, it's perhaps because we find it hard to view ourselves first and foremost as citizens of heaven; for the lament of those who dwell on the earth in chapter 18 gives way to the joy of heaven when Babylon falls.

We might find it hard to imagine seeing things this way, but God cares more for the life of his people (v 19-20) than he does for all the trade that an economy can generate.

⌄ Apply

❓ *Look back at the letters to Smyrna (2:9) and Laodicea (3:17). What have the people in chapter 18 failed to understand?*

❓ *Why would it have been very easy for Christians to simply "join in" with the values and systems of the day?*

❓ *How would this vision of judgment help Christians to see where the path of faithful Christian witness lies?*

❓ *How might it help you?*

This is the end that is coming to all human cultures. Read through the passage again, if you dare, and substitute the name of your own country for Babylon. International trade brings huge benefit to people—who can conceive of a life without tea, coffee or sugar? But it also has a downside in the use and abuse of people—human souls (see 18:13). It is sobering to realise that heaven, disgusted by the injustice and persecution that these systems generate, will rejoice over silent factories and empty shopping centres.

⌃ Pray

Ask the Lord to help you see the world as he sees it, and know what true wealth is.

Pray for those who fight against injustice in the system: the police, judiciary and other agencies that bring relief.

Heaven's song

Every act in the drama of the book of Revelation is accompanied by worship in heaven…

The angel announced the judgment of God to the world at the end of chapter 18. Now we are invited to listen to heaven's playlist.

Read Revelation 19:1-5

❷ Whose voices do we hear?
❷ What does each voice represent?
❷ What are we meant to take from the fact that they are united in their view?
❷ What is the essential and important distinction that is made by the voices from heaven (v 1-2)?

The voices of the redeemed (the multitude, v 1), representatives of the old and new covenants (the 24 elders, v 4), and finally a voice from the throne, all see Rome for what it truly is. Only God's judgment is true and just (v 2). Rome (the great prostitute, v 2) was feared and admired in equal measure by its enemies, and was a source of immense pride and glory to its members and citizens. Our modern cultures still look back to imperial Rome as the measure of greatness. Our governments and universities have senate buildings; our architecture uses pillars to denote both authority and permanence.

But God's verdict is the opposite. Great it may have been, but when Rome sets itself up as God, and murders and oppresses the true citizens of heaven, then its fate is sealed. Rome thought it was civilising; God sees it is corrupting (v 2).

⌄ Apply

❷ *What is it about your own culture or country that people take pride in?*
❷ *How valuable does heaven think that is?*
❷ *What things do you particularly feel proud about for your country?*
❷ *Why should we be suspicious of those feelings and instincts?*

Cultures, rulers and countries cannot help but try to attract glory to themselves. It's an instinctive way to build up leaders and to manipulate citizens. We do it with stirring songs and feel-good images that say, "We're important", "We're special", "We're better than those other people over there". But Christians should beware all these beguiling messages. We need to tune ourselves in to the songs of heaven, not the jingoistic tunes of earth. And when we understand the verdict of heaven on our particular patch of the world, we should join with the voices of verse 4 and say "Amen, Hallelujah!"

God alone deserves our praise.

⌃ Pray

Respond in your own way to the command from the throne in verse 5.

Is there something in your attitude to your country, or any particular group you belong to, that you need to repent of?

Wedding song

This last half of Revelation could be described as a tale of two women. On the one hand we have the powerful controlling state who is depicted as a great prostitute.

On the other hand there is a beautiful bride who is preparing herself for a wedding.

The invitation

Read Revelation 19:6-8

> ❷ Who picks up the call from the throne to praise God in verse 5?
> ❷ How does verse 6 indicate the mood of these people?
> ❷ Who is the bride?
> ❷ What is the significance of the bride's clothing and how she got it?

Instead of receiving an invitation from a prostitute (17:1), we're invited to be the bride of God's Son (19:6-7). Instead of seeing a woman clothed in the purple of empire (17:4), we see a bride clothed in the fine linen of righteous deeds (19:8; Isaiah 61:10). Instead of receiving an invitation to immorality (Revelation 17:2), we're invited to a pure wedding (19:7). Note that the clothing is "given [to] her". She is the bride by the grace of God.

Who is truly blessed?

Read Revelation 19:9-10

> ❷ What is the message that the angel wants to impress upon John and upon us?
> ❷ Why might John have made the mistake in verse 10?

> ❷ What do we learn about the status of angels in verse 10?
> ❷ What do you think the final statement of verse 10 means?

The angel says to John, "Write this". John presumably has been feverishly scribbling down everything he's seen and heard. But this part of the vision must not be missed: "Blessed are those who are invited to the wedding supper of the Lamb!" So great and gracious is this message that the angel feels compelled to add, "These are the true words of God". In other words, *I'm not making this up!* And so great and gracious is this message that John worships the messenger, earning himself a forthright angelic rebuke. The final phrase in verse 10 is intriguing, but surely it means that any prophetic word that is given must accord with the known testimony about who Jesus was and is. And the reverse is also true. Whoever speaks the gospel message about Jesus is "prophesying"—speaking the words of God to others.

⌄ Apply

> ❷ What do you count as more significant: the honour and reputation you have in this world or the fact that you will be bound to Jesus for eternity?
> ❷ Is that reflected in the way you:
> • think about others?
> • speak about yourself?
> • pray?

Reigning rider

This section starts the final set of sevens in Revelation, which is indicated by the words "I saw heaven standing open…"

Previously, we have had bowls and seals and trumpets that follow the same general pattern. The first five describe life now or in history; the sixth describes the judgment; the seventh describes what lies beyond. This is no different. Each of the seven visions start with a version of "I saw…"

The ruler rides out
Read Revelation 19:11-16

❓ *What details about the rider let us know who this is referring to?*
❓ *What does the rider do in the world?*
❓ *What aspects of his work do you find difficult to reconcile with your view of him?*

People often associate this section with the return of Christ. Here, however, Christ rides forth on a horse rather than returning on the clouds. He is described in verse 12 in language that closely echoes the vision of Christ walking among the first-century churches of Asia Minor (1:14). His robe is dipped in the blood of sacrifice, and his weapon is "the Word of God". Christ reigns now through the gospel. This is how he extends his kingdom and defeats his enemies. His army is the missionary church (v 14). The risen Christ is given all authority over the nations, and so he sends forth his disciples to call the nations to obedience to his teaching.

The call to harvest
Read Revelation 19:17-18

❓ *What gruesome invitation does the angel give? What does this represent?*

All mission is an act of "gathering". When people respond positively, we gather them for salvation, but when they reject our message, we gather them for judgment. One way or another, our gospel proclamation prepares people for eternity.

The victor in battle
Read Revelation 19:19-21

❓ *What does this battle represent?*
❓ *Who wins, and how?*
❓ *What becomes of the enemy?*
❓ *What encouragement should this be to us as we bear testimony to Jesus in everyday life?*

The conflict between the people of Christ and the people of the beast intensifies before the final judgment of the beast (v 20) and the defeat of its followers (v 21). Those who oppose God's people may look terrifying, and as though they are winning. But we can be confident that they will lose to our mighty warrior King. The weapon is the word of God.

❓ *How does this make you feel about your Bible? And about this world?*

Bible in a year: Jonah • Matthew 5 v 27-48 ✓

Goodness is good

Proverbs is effectively a training guide for life, for living life to the full. Contrary to popular opinion, Proverbs believes that goodness is good for you...

As you slowly and carefully read this rather random collection of proverbs, use this version of the Swedish Bible-study method to focus your thoughts:

1. Draw a *light bulb* next to the proverb that "shines" and draws your attention.

2. Draw a *question mark* against something that, at first sight, seems difficult to understand.

3. Place an *arrow* next to the proverb that you think personally applies to you right now.

4. Put a *speech bubble* with a name in it next to the proverb of someone who you think would benefit from hearing about what you discovered in that verse.

Read Proverbs 10:13-22

Light-bulb proverb

❓ *What was it that drew your attention?*
❓ *How is the thought new to you, or different from how you have seen it expressed before?*
❓ *What are you going to do about it?*

I was drawn to verse 19, and the observation that when I am in the wrong, I tend to talk a lot and try to explain my way out of it. It is a cautionary warning to me. All my words cannot wash away sins. Only *the* Word, Jesus, can. Stop talking, Tim, and confess.

Question-mark proverb

❓ *What is it that you don't "get"?*

Spend a couple of minutes thinking imaginatively about the situation it might be written for.

❓ *Has it become clearer?*

We are meant to take our time reading and pondering these proverbs—in that way, they are a bit like mini parables. If the meaning is still opaque, ask a fellow Christian to make a suggestion,

Arrow proverb

❓ *What are you going to do, specifically, as a result of reading this proverb?*

Speech-bubble proverb

❓ *Why do you think this might be appropriate to share with your friend?*
❓ *What are you hoping will result from this conversation?*

▲ Pray

Pray that your friend will have open ears to receive what you humbly share with them from this passage.

Praise God for the truth of verse 16.

Satan is bound

This is the fourth, and therefore the central, vision of this last cycle. How we understand its meaning will shape how we think about the world and the future.

Read Revelation 20:1-6

❷ *What explanations have you heard about the meaning of the millennium pictured in these verses?*

❷ *Think about each element of what happens in this vision. How might these fit into what we have already read in Revelation?*

These verses not only describe a battle but have *been* a battlefield of debate between Christians over the years. There are different ways of reading them, depending on whether you take them to be describing a sequential series of events that take place in the future, or symbolic of something that is happening throughout history. There are three main views (with many variations):

Premillennialism: Premillennialists believe that Christ will return before (pre-) the millennium. He will then reign on earth for a literal thousand-year period. Christ will be physically present on earth and reign as its King, bringing peace and prosperity, with believers reigning alongside him. The thousand-year reign of Christ will end with the great battle of Armageddon, after which the final judgment will take place.

Postmillennialism: Postmillennialists believe that Christ returns after (post-) the millennium. They believe the millennium is a future golden age of gospel advance in which the church grows and exercises a positive influence in society. After this golden age, Christ will return and the final judgment will take place. Postmillennialists generally have a positive view of history. History is improving as the gospel advances.

Amillennialism: Amillennialists do believe there is a millennium. But it's not in the future. Instead they see the millennium as describing the present age of the church. The millennium is therefore the period between the first and second comings of Christ. Amillennialists interpret Revelation 20 in the light of the broader picture presented in the Scriptures.

❷ *Which of these views do you generally hold to, if any?*

❷ *Putting aside the precise meaning of these verses, what are some "big picture" truths about God and Satan that are woven through this vision?*

❷ *Who will be blessed and why (v 6)?*

⌃ Pray

Ask the Lord to help you understand the meaning of these verses.

Pray that those in your church, or other churches, who take different views on this would respect and love each other, and unite in the task of making Christ known.

Rejoice that God is in control, and that the work of the evil one is restrained.

More on this tomorrow...

Thousand-year reign

Yesterday we looked at some different ways in which Christians have understood the millennium. Today we focus on one view, and how we should respond.

Read Revelation 20:1-6

❓ *What incidents or teaching in the rest of the New Testament come to mind when you think about Satan being "bound" or his activity restricted?*

···· **TIME OUT** ···································

Read the following Bible passages and reflect on how they might impact our understanding of what is being described in Revelation 20:

Mark 3:26-27

John 12:31

1 John 3:8

Matthew 16:18-19

Colossians 2:14-15

2 Thessalonians 2:1-8

·······································

I take Revelation 20:1-6 to be a reference to the defeat of Satan at the cross and resurrection. In John 12:31 Jesus says that "now"—that is, through his impending death and resurrection—"the prince of this world will be driven out". In summary, the cross and resurrection have limited for a period Satan's power to deceive to create the opportunity for the church's mission to the nations.

It might not always seem as if Satan is bound, as we see him vent his fury against God's people (Revelation 12:17). But consider this: for centuries God's kingdom on earth was confined to one small nation, and they were rarely faithful to him. But since the cross, the message of Christ has spread across the globe, and millions of people have been added to his kingdom.

⌄ Apply

Surely John would not want our response to be one of arguing about the detail! The big-picture teaching and responses are:

- *Confidence:* God is more powerful than Satan. At every moment in this narrative, God is in control.

- *Privilege:* Those who belong to Christ reign with Christ. We are encouraged to remain faithful and to resist worshipping the beast because of our status.

- *Perseverance:* Even those who have been beheaded for remaining faithful to Christ will reign with him (20:4). We are encouraged to bear the testimony of Jesus and the word of God.

⌃ Pray

Shape your prayers around the three points above.

✓ *Bible in a year: 1 Kings 6-7 • Matthew 7*

Final battle

Throughout Revelation "1,000" is symbolic of "many". John is describing the "many" years of history between the first and second comings of Christ.

Again, John uses highly pictorial language, picking up images from the Old Testament to describe the intensifying struggle between God and his people and the forces of darkness, which precedes the end.

Read Revelation 20:7-10

❷ *How might the situation look up to the middle of verse 9?*

❷ *What is the result of the battle?*

❷ *What Old Testament references or allusions come to mind here?*

❷ *What becomes of Satan and those who follow him in the end?*

It looks like a catastrophe: Satan on the loose; the forces of evil all over the earth; God's people surrounded by an enemy so numerous that they are like the sand on the seashore. In Ezekiel 38 – 39 the prophet speaks symbolically of Gog and Magog. Magog was a name from Israel's ancient history (Genesis 10:1-2), and in Ezekiel they represent all those throughout history who have opposed God and his people.

But in Revelation 20, now comes the sudden reversal. Just as when Elijah stood alone against hundreds of prophets of Baal (2 Kings 1:10-14), the terrifying battle is over at a stroke from heaven. As threatening and terrifying as the enemy look, they are *nothing* compared to the power of God.

☑ Apply

❷ *What are the forces that oppose Christ, his church and the gospel message that make you fearful?*

❷ *How does this part of Revelation 20 encourage you to think differently about them?*

❷ *Why should verse 10 lead us to rejoice?*

Watching for signs

This fifth vision provides a transition to the end of history described in the sixth vision. It suggests that at the end of the church age, prior to the return of Christ, the restraints placed upon Satan will to some extent be released (see 2 Thessalonians 2:7), and the conflict between the kingdoms of Christ and Satan will intensify. Some people use this observation to make claims about the imminence of the return of Christ today.

❷ *What claims have you heard along these lines in recent years? Do you know anyone who talks about this?*

❷ *What should our attitude towards reading signs like this be?*

We should be wary of using world events as a predictive tool, since Christ says no one knows when he will return (Mark 13:32), and the apostles spoke of his return as always potentially imminent.

The great white throne

The fifth vision began, "I saw thrones..." (v 4); the sixth begins, "Then I saw a great white throne..." (v 11).

As you read today's passage slowly, focus on the emotions and feelings you have as each part of the scene is described.

Read Revelation 20:11-15

❓ *How is it made clear that everyone will be judged?*

❓ *What do the different books contain?*

❓ *What is the basis for judgment, which is applied to everyone?*

❓ *Does this feel like threat to you, or a relief to you, or both?*

Christ returns to judge the living and the dead. The defeat of Satan in verses 7-10 leads to the final judgment. The language makes it clear that there will be no one who does not appear before the great white throne of God's judgment. Great and small—kings and emperors together with children. Death, Hades and the sea all give up their dead—not a single person will be left out. All will be raised to life to face the judgment on the last day. Christians are not meant to feel threatened by this, but rather, encouraged. Not a single person who has done harm to another will escape the consequences. Even the first death will not be an escape for them, because everyone will be raised to life to face judgment.

Two kinds of books are involved in the final judgment. First, the annals of history are opened because people are judged according to what they have done (v 12-13).

If that were the sole basis of judgment, then we would *all* be condemned. But second, a further book is opened—the Lamb's book of life, listing everyone saved by the Lamb's sacrificial death.

⌄ Apply

❓ *How should this understanding change the way we think about people who are not Christians?*

❓ *How should this passage change the way we think about injustice and evil in the world?*

❓ *How can we know if our names are written in the Lamb's book of life?*

Revelation's answer to the last question is to look at the evidence of our lives. Are we bearing the testimony of Jesus? Are we being faithful, even if it means suffering and death? Do we hate what God hates? Do we love what God loves?

❓ *If you were arrested for being a Christian, would there be enough evidence to convict you? What would that evidence be?*

⌃ Pray

Talk to the Lord about your friends, family and acquaintances. Ask God to have mercy on them, and to give you the opportunity to share the testimony of Jesus with them before they gather with you before the great white throne.

The new creation

John reaches the climax of his book. And what a climax! There are many surprises in these last two chapters that explode the views of heaven in our culture.

But before we start, take a moment to think.

❓ *What do you imagine eternity will be like?*
❓ *What are you most looking forward to?*
❓ *When was the last time you talked with a fellow Christian about eternity?*

Heaven and earth

Read Revelation 21:1-4

❓ *What is described as new in these verses?*
❓ *What has passed away?*
❓ *How is this different to many of the ideas about heaven that are around in our culture (and even among Christians)?*

We will not be ethereal spirits floating on clouds and playing harps; we will have bodies. This description of eternity is remarkable for its *physicality*. Nor do we go *up* to heaven! Heaven in a sense comes down to earth, in a uniting of the spiritual and physical realms.

⌄ Apply

This is why it is actually more accurate to talk about being in the new creation for eternity, rather than "going to heaven". Being kept safe in heaven is only a temporary measure before the new creation comes into being. Many flights from the UK to Australia stop off in Singapore, but when you board the flight in London, you do not

say, "I'm going to Singapore". You say, "I'm going to Australia".

❓ *How will you need to think and speak differently about eternity from now on?*

The heart of heaven

Although what follows in Revelation 21 is a description of something that is physical, it is laden with symbols. There are things about eternity that are impossible to convey in words. We are being encouraged to let our imaginations run riot!

❓ *But what is at the heart of the new creation (v 3)?*
❓ *What images and references from the rest of the Bible does verse 3 make you think about?*

John wants us to think about the covenant that God first established with his people in the Old Testament. **Read Genesis 17:3-4; Exodus 6:7; Ezekiel 34:24; Jeremiah 7:23.** What is being realised in the new creation is God's plan from the dawn of time in the garden, and throughout history.

⌄ Apply

❓ *What excites you about what you have read today?*

Take the opportunity to talk to someone about your hope today.

An end to suffering

Perhaps we are not quite so excited about the new creation because so many of us have things relatively easy.

The wedding
Read Revelation 21:1-4

❓ *What had the first readers of Revelation been experiencing?*

❓ *How different was their experience to that of ours?*

❓ *How different is ours to that of other Christians from around the world?*

❓ *Why might the words of verses 3-4 be so comforting to them?*

❓ *How do you feel as you read, and begin to imagine, the promise at the start of verse 4?*

To a group of people who were being threatened or under active persecution for their faith in Christ, these verses would surely have brought tears of joy. I wonder if sometimes, for those of us who are living in comfort, we forget how deeply distressing, emotionally painful and physically challenging persecution can be—both back then and here now. There are parts of the world today where Christians are imprisoned, murdered or pushed from their homes. Families are torn apart. People lose all their possessions. How utterly wonderful to know that God is waiting at the end to welcome them, and *personally* to dry their eyes from the very real agonies they have gone through for his name's sake.

Pray

Ask the Lord to comfort those who are suffering now with this reassurance.

What's missing?
Re-read Revelation 21:4

❓ *What things are listed in verse 4 that will be completely absent in the new creation?*

❓ *Which of these things have you experienced yourself in the past?*

❓ *Which are you experiencing most now?*

❓ *How do you respond to the promises at the end of verse 4?*

There will be no hearses, no hospitals and no need for handkerchiefs in eternity. The reasons for weeping in sorrow have been removed for ever. Decay and death are part of a world under God's curse because of the fall. Remember that death itself was thrown into the lake of fire (20:14). Now that all things have been made new, they are a thing of the past.

Apply

❓ *How might you use these words to comfort someone who is weeping now because of illness or bereavement?*

❓ *How can you ensure that this thought is in the front of your mind when you weep over loss of some kind?*

Solid as a rock

As we grow in our understanding of God's word and his ways, one great result is that we become more consistent as Christians and are better able to weather the storms of life.

Shaken

Before you read the passage, think:

❓ *When have you most struggled to be stable and consistent as a Christian?*

❓ *What event or experience has most shaken you as a Christian? How did you get through that time?*

Read Proverbs 10:23-32

Imagine you were reading these words during one of the times you thought about above.

❓ *What advice would you give yourself from them about how to persevere as a Christian through difficult times?*

It is intriguing that Proverbs does not hesitate to tell us about the downside of rejecting God's ways. When our faith is shaky for some reason, we can easily start to envy those who are not Christians. It becomes a struggle and an effort to walk with the Lord in the paths of righteousness. By contrast, our non-Christian friends can seem to have relatively easy and carefree lives.

⋯ TIME OUT ⋯

Read Psalm 73

❓ *Do the thoughts in verses 4-14 resonate with you?*

❓ *What (and from where) did the psalmist discover the truths that helped him out of his dilemma (v 17-20, 23-26)?*

We need to remember that *time* is not *eternity*. What might look like one thing now is revealed to be another when we see it from heaven's perspective. The way of the ungodly inevitably leads to death. The way of the righteous inevitably leads to life. You may feel that your life is shaky but, if you are in Christ, your feet are planted on the solid rock, and you will stand firm as others are swept away (Proverbs 10:25).

Stirred

Read Proverbs 10:32

❓ *What contrast is being drawn here?*

❓ *What is it encouraging us to do?*

When I have known times of shaky faith, it has been the honest and plain-speaking encouragement of Christian friends that has helped the most. They have reminded me of truths that I have forgotten to remember. They have reminded me that, in Christ, I have received the words of eternal life, and that I have nowhere else to go (and need nowhere else to go). They have reminded me that the life that finds favour with God is a life lived in faithful, dependent trust on God's word and God's ways.

✔ Apply

❓ *In what way could you be an honest, plain-speaking Christian friend to someone today?*

All things new

The new creation will be perfect: free from sin, death and suffering of any kind. But it will also be free from anyone who can spoil it...

Read Revelation 21:5-8

In and out

❓ *What are the qualifications of those that enter the new creation?*
❓ *What is promised to them (v 7)?*
❓ *Who will be excluded (v 8)?*
❓ *What will become of them instead?*

As with many of the lists of sins in the New Testament, it's very easy to notice those we are not guilty of, and feel comfortable. We may not have been sorcerers, murderers or sexually immoral. But let us be honest: who of us can claim that we have not been cowardly, or faithless at times, or have not told lies when it has suited us? On such a reading, the lake of fire is the destination for all of us.

By grace

❓ *What promises in verses 6-7 give us hope?*
❓ *How might you explain this to someone who is fearful that they are "not good enough for heaven"?*
❓ *Are there any conditions (v 7)?*

Of course, none of us are good enough for heaven. But these verses make clear that it is the gospel of grace that brings us into right relationship with God. Those who trust in Christ are adopted into God's family and are privileged to be called his sons (v 7).

But the word from the one seated on the throne makes it clear that this is a promise for those who "are victorious". In fact, all the way through Revelation we are reminded that the sure promise is given to those who, through God's strength, endure, are faithful and bear the testimony of Jesus. "Be faithful, even to the point of death," says the Lord Jesus to his people in Smyrna, "and I will give you life as your victor's crown" (Revelation 2:10).

✔ Apply

We must be careful how we listen to, and repeat to others, what might appear to be competing commands and promises. If we are tempted to give in (or, indeed, have already given in) to the pressures around us, we need to clearly hear Jesus saying to us, "Be faithful, even to the point of death". We need to hear him say to us that no liars will be present in the new creation.

But when we are feeling weak and vulnerable—when we are crying out to God because it is hard, or when endurance seems too much, or when our lives are spinning out of control—we need to hear his word of invitation and comfort: "To the thirsty I will give water without cost from the spring of the water of life" (21:6).

❓ *Which of these do you need to hear now?*
❓ *Which message could you share with a Christian friend today?*

Bridal building

An angel arrives to show John the bride, the wife of the lamb. But what he shows him is not a woman resplendent in a wedding dress but something different... a city.

Read Revelation 21:9-14

❓ *Where does this "bride-city" come from? What is the significance of that?*

❓ *What aspects of this city does John want us to take note of in verse 11?*

❓ *What is symbolically important about the description in verses 12-14?*

❓ *Why do you think the number 12 is repeated so often here?*

The redeemed people of God come from heaven to earth (21:2, 10). This is a picture of those who belong to Christ coming "down" from heaven to the renewed earth. This picks up on what the New Testament teaches elsewhere. "For you died, and your life is now hidden with Christ in God" (Colossians 3:3). "And God raised us up with Christ and seated us with him in the heavenly realms in Christ Jesus" (Ephesians 2:6). When Christ returns, our true selves, which are in some mysterious sense already in heaven with Christ, will be revealed in all their resurrection-body fullness.

In Revelation 21:11 the temple-city shines with the glory of God like a jewel. It is literally *brilliant!* The Jerusalem temple had a single entrance. In verses 12-13 the temple-city has gates on all four sides because people enter from the four corners of the world (see Isaiah 60:11; Ezekiel 48:30-34).

In the ancient world benefactors often had their names inscribed on the public works they had funded. We have something similar today in foundation stones inscribed with the names of the dignitaries who laid them. According to Revelation 21:14, the temple-city has twelve foundations inscribed with the names of the apostles who laid them. This is a reference to the apostolic testimony we have in the New Testament (Ephesians 2:19-20). The church is created by the word and secured by the word.

⌄ Apply

Where are you now? In one sense, you are sitting in a chair reading this at home or on a train. But in another, more real sense, you are already seated with Christ in heaven, awaiting the moment when Christ is revealed to the world for who he truly is.

What are you now? You may think of yourself as relatively unimportant, with little to offer in the grand scheme of things. You may be conscious of failing health or think you have very little to contribute or give. In reality your true self is glorious and brilliant. Together with your brothers and sisters in Christ, you bathe in the brilliance of the glory of God and share in his shining like a precious jewel. That is who you truly are.

Walk tall today, confident in who you are in Christ by the grace of God.

Evaluating eternity

What's the biggest building you've ever seen? The Shard in London, the Empire State in New York, or the CN Tower in Toronto are tiny compared to the new Jerusalem...

Read Revelation 21:15-21

❓ *What is staggering about the dimensions of the city?*

❓ *What are we meant to take from the symbolic description of the materials that this cube-shaped city is made up from?*

❓ *How might this lavish description be a comfort and encouragement to those to whom John first wrote?*

❓ *How are they an encouragement to you?*

The measurements are deeply symbolic (see Ezekiel 40 – 43; Zechariah 2:1-2). 12,000 stadia is 12 (a picture of the complete people of God because of the 12 tribes and 12 apostles) times 1,000 (a picture of a multitude). 12,000 stadia is around 1,400 miles (2,200 kilometres). This is a massive city for it contains all God's redeemed people. It's about the size of the world as it was then known. The width of the wall, 144 cubits, is twelve squared. It's perhaps a reference to the testimony of the prophets and the twelve apostles, who make the church secure. 144 cubits is 72 yards (65 metres). Massively thick walls. The point is clear: once-persecuted Christians will be eternally secure within these walls. This security is reinforced by the presence of angelic watchmen on every gate in Revelation 21:12 (Isaiah 62:6).

The city is not only 1,400 miles square; it's also 1,400 miles tall. Everest is about six miles tall, so 1,400 miles takes us out beyond earth's atmosphere! Again, it's clearly symbolic. This cube echoes the Most Holy Place in Solomon's temple (1 Kings 6:20), which was a cube. The whole city is the Most Holy Place, where God meets with his people. In the past only the high priest could enter and only once a year and only through the shedding of blood. But the curtain barring entrance was torn in two as Jesus died (Mark 15:38). The blood of Jesus has opened the way, and we follow him into the super-cubed holy presence of God (Hebrews 10:19-22).

In the original temple, the jewels on the priest's breastplate represented the tribes of Israel, which he symbolically brought into God's presence (Exodus 28:17-20). Here those same jewels are embedded into the fabric of the temple-city (Revelation 21:18-21). The city is paved with gold (v 21), just as the temple was coated in gold. The value of pearls in the ancient world was so great that a single pearl earring once financed an entire war. The description is meant to overwhelm us with its extravagant richness.

⌄ Apply

Do you consider yourself poor? You are not. The vast and unimaginable wealth of God is part of your inheritance in Christ.

Do you consider yourself wealthy? If this is driven by an evaluation of your human wealth, think again. If you are in Christ, then your true wealth awaits you in eternity.

What's missing?

We have already seen that crying, grief and pain will be absent in the new creation. John now focuses on some more things that are missing...

Redundant

Read Revelation 21:22-27

❓ *What four things are missing from the new Jerusalem?*

❓ *What is the significance of each thing mentioned that will be absent?*

❓ *What is the significance of verse 26, do you think?*

There is no temple. There is no need for separation or sacrifice. Everyone has access to the Father and the Son. In fact, the new Jerusalem is described almost like a gigantic Most Holy Place—the place where God dwells.

No sun or moon. We have no need of their light because God is present to light our path.

No night / the gates are always open. In a human city closed gates were necessary to prevent intruders and the dark deeds that were done at night. There is no need for that because evil of all kinds has been dealt with.

Nothing impure. Verse 27 can feel like a warning. But it's primarily a promise. Nothing will enter the city that can spoil it. Although this does speak to judgment, it primarily means that eternity can never be a re-run of the first Eden, which was ruined through the presence of the snake. We can be confident that eternity will be unspoiled for ever.

There is no room for sin (v 27), but the glory and wealth of the nations will somehow be brought in and incorporated into the new creation. This suggests that there is some kind of continuity between old and new creations; and there is redeemable value in aspects of our human art and culture.

⌄ Apply

❓ *When do you feel like giving up following Christ?*

❓ *What in John's vision of the new Jerusalem captures your imagination or speaks to your current challenges?*

❓ *How should John's vision of the possibility of redeemed culture shape your attitude towards life now?*

⌃ Pray

Scan your eyes over chapter 21, and then spend some time thanking and praising God for all that awaits you.

Ask God to help you to be faithful to the end.

Eden restored

John's final vision ends with the words at the start of chapter 22. And what astonishing words they are…

Restored

Read Revelation 22:1-2

❓ Where does the river come from and what does it do?

❓ What does this picture bring to mind from elsewhere in the Bible? (Hint: Read Genesis 2:9-10.)

❓ What does John want us to understand about eternity from this description?

We're still in the city, but now it's not a temple-city but a garden-city. This is the Garden of Eden restored (with imagery drawn from Ezekiel's vision of a new temple in Ezekiel 47). A river flows through the garden-city just as a river flowed through Eden. The river feeds a tree (Revelation 22:2). The fact that the single tree is located on both banks reminds us that this is symbolic. "The water of life" feeds "the tree of life". And the tree not only sustains life; it also *restores* life, for its leaves heal the nations. It produces twelve crops each year—it constantly gives life to God's people.

The key thing in this imagery is that this life-giving river flows from the throne of God and the Lamb. Ultimately it is the Lamb who gives life. And the fact that Jesus is described as the Lamb indicates that this life comes through his death. Christians do not become immortal in the sense of having a self-sustaining life. Instead we live for ever because we are for ever given life through the death of Jesus.

Relationship

Read Revelation 22:3-4

Eden was a place of failure and shame that led to God's curse upon mankind. In Genesis 3:24 angels blocked the way back to Eden, because God's presence was dangerous to people who were now sinful. But now we belong to him and see him face to face.

Reigning

Read Revelation 22:5

❓ What do you think will be involved in "reigning with God?

It is hard to know what this will be like—presumably, we will return to the original Genesis mandate to subdue the world (and the universe) and fill it to the praise of God's glory. That may involve exploration, industry and creativity, but the symbolic nature of the description here should make us hesitant to be too definitive about what eternity will be like. But we do know it will involve our flourishing and fulfilment, both personally and in community with all God's people.

⌃ Pray

Spend some time thinking about who you are: a servant and a worshipper but also a co-heir with Christ. Praise God for who you are in Christ, and for what awaits you.

Keeping the book

"And they will reign with him for ever and ever" are the final words of the revelation given to John, and the climactic promise of the book. But there is more to be said.

Soon and very soon
Read Revelation 22:6-7

❷ What phrase from verse 7 is repeated in verse 12?

❷ How could this be true when John wrote Revelation 2,000 years ago?

❷ Why do you think Christ has not yet returned?

Jesus is coming "soon". But he has not yet come—after 2,000 years. Christians are meant to live knowing and thinking Christ will return at any moment, at just the right time. Every day he delays is another day of mercy and gospel opportunity. Every day he delays, more people are being brought into his kingdom. We are called to be patient, and to remember that with the Lord a thousand years are as a day (2 Peter 3:8).

✔ Apply

The fact that Jesus is coming "soon" has led some Christians to withdraw from engagement with the world. What's the point, they suppose, of being involved in bringing change when it will all be soon swept away? But we are called to love our neighbour while we wait for Christ's return. And the return of Christ should drive us towards evangelism, for every day he delays is a day of opportunity and mercy.

❷ How will Jesus' return shape your day today?

Life goes on
Read Revelation 22:7-11

❷ What promises are given in verse 7, and by whom?

❷ Why might John, again, be tempted to worship the angel?

❷ What rebuke does he receive in response?

❷ What do you think the enigmatic statements in verse 11 mean?

These words are to be kept. Jesus himself speaks in verse 7 and calls on us as readers to "[keep] the words". What does this involve? The next incident highlights the key message. John bows in worship before the angel (v 8) but is rebuked for this idolatry. The command is "Worship God!" (v 9). This goes to the core of Revelation. We're to worship God in the face of both the seductions and threat of idolatrous power—and to do so intelligently. Even though the angel would have been impressive, astonishing and glorious, an angel is not worthy of our worship—only God is.

The words are to be read. Daniel was told to seal up his prophecy, for it described a future time (Daniel 12:4, 9). By contrast, John is told *not* to seal the scroll, for "the time is near". In other words, this is not a message for some far-off future. This is for John's generation (Revelation 22:10)—and therefore also for ours. Life goes on (v 11), but we are to continue worshipping and faithfully sharing Jesus as we wait for his return.

Watch your weights

Proverbs shows us that living God's way is not just about having a "spiritual" mindset. True godliness is as practical as potatoes.

Commercial returns

Read Proverbs 11:1

❷ *What situation in the marketplace does this proverb relate to?*
❷ *Why are people tempted to do this?*
❷ *Beyond weighing scales and short-changing people, what general principle does this proverb point to?*

Spend a moment thinking about all the ways that this lack of basic honesty and integrity pervades much commercial life and our relationships with others.

❷ *Why do you think the LORD "detests" this?*

Cheating people out of what has been promised to them is the same as using scales that have been tampered with. We see it in advertising that promises the world but delivers something cheap and shoddy. It basically comes down to stealing and lying. It's why it's good business advice to reverse this strategy and (if anything) under-promise but over-deliver.

God loves truth and integrity because these qualities are of his essence. So too is justice. When these proverbs were first written, unscrupulous traders would use dishonest scales to cheat people out of what was rightfully theirs—perhaps even robbing the poor who came to them to buy grain. When we cheat the poor and vulnerable, we need to know that we are exploiting people whom God loves to defend and champion. Beware.

The fall

Read Proverbs 11:2

❷ *Why will pride lead to disgrace?*
❷ *How does humility lead to wisdom?*
❷ *Can you think of examples of these two principles in your own life?*

It seems ridiculously obvious to say that you cannot learn unless you admit your ignorance. And yet, for all kinds of reasons, we often fall into the trap of believing that saving face is preferable to learning more. When people are filled with pride in their own importance and abilities, they are simply laying themselves open to making mistakes or having their inadequacies discovered. Their sense of self-importance makes the experience of being disgraced all the harder to bear.

❷ *How is this verse true in eternity?*

Having pride in ourselves before God is idiotic. The only sensible attitude before almighty God, our Creator and Judge, is to kneel humbly before him. Only then will we learn and grow.

⌄ Apply

Read 1 Peter 5:5-6

Come to the Lord humbly, asking him to help you to know him and to grow in him.

 Bible in a year: 2 Kings 13-14 • Matthew 14 v 1-21

Waiting for his coming

What will the return of Jesus mean for humankind?

....

Read Revelation 22:12-16

❓ *What will Jesus do when he returns (v 12)?*

❓ *What is the meaning of each of the descriptions the Lord Jesus gives of himself in verses 13 and 16 (we've seen all of them previously in Revelation!)?*

❓ *How is the gospel of grace shown in these verses?*

❓ *What warnings are there here for us to heed?*

These words are gospel. Revelation 21:8 and 27 have warned that not everyone enters the temple-garden-city. 22:15 reiterates this. Jesus will reward everyone "according to what they have done" (v 12). So what hope is there for guilty sinners? "Blessed are those who wash their robes, that they may have the right to the tree of life and may go through the gates into the city" (v 14). Our hope is not in our righteousness. Our hope is in Christ, who is the Alpha and the Omega.

By faith, we wash our guilty stains in his blood and clothe ourselves with his right-eousness. "I am the Root and the Offspring of David, and the bright Morning Star" (v 16). In other words, Jesus is the promised Messiah, the son of David who receives David's authority. The Morning Star is also a messianic title (see Numbers 24:17).

The mighty Lord of creation will come both to reward but also to judge.

✔ Apply

This is the Jesus we worship: the One who waits to be revealed from heaven to all humankind. And we must work to keep the full picture of who he is in our minds. Depending on our situation, we can default to thinking of Christ in one of several unbalanced ways. Perhaps we emphasise his grace, mercy and love, and dial down the volume on the fact that he will be the judge; or perhaps we glory in his justice (as we ought to) but assume his love and grace are limited in some way.

❓ *When are you in danger of losing sight of who Jesus truly is?*

❓ *Have you ever despaired of Jesus coming "soon"?*

❓ *How can we help ourselves to keep believing in and living in light of his return?*

⌃ Pray

Pray that you and all your fellow believers would believe and know the truth of verse 14.

Famous last words

John finishes his book with some profound and powerful words—and a prayer that rounds off the final chapter of our Bibles.

The end

Read Revelation 22:18-19

❓ *What do you think it might mean to "add" something to the words of the prophecy?*

❓ *What kinds of things might we be tempted to "take away" from them?*

❓ *Why do you think this is taken so seriously?*

These words are final. Verses 18-19 warn us against ignoring the book of Revelation *and* extrapolating from John's words so that they say something different to what he intended. We are not at liberty to dial down the reality of God's judgment, or to overemphasise one truth at the expense of another. This is *God's* revelation, and we are to be faithful to it. What is at stake is our eternity and the destiny of those around us.

But throughout the history of the church, these words have often been interpreted as an affirmation that the canon of Scripture is now closed (just as the Law of Moses was closed, Deuteronomy 4:2). To add to John's words is to add to Scripture. So John warns that no one will receive a message from God that has the authority of Scripture. No book can be added to our Bibles—that includes the Qur'an, the Book of Mormon and any prophecy that claims to supplement or supplant the Bible. So explicit is Revelation 22:18-19 on this that to claim another source of divine revelation is to deny John's

revelation. I would go so far as to say that you can't find hope in what John says about our share in the tree of life while at the same time denying what John says about the close of the canon.

The final test

Read Revelation 22:17, 20-21

❓ *What thought does John want to leave us with?*

❓ *How does his final prayer summarise the message of the book?*

We might think of this as the final "test" in Revelation. Jesus says, "I am coming soon". Do we respond with an enthusiastic "Amen"? Do we pray this prayer? Do we long for Christ's return? Or are our longings elsewhere? Would we prefer his return to be postponed? If so, this may be a sign that we need to "come out" of Babylon (18:4).

So through Christ, the invitation comes to us from the Spirit, speaking through the church ("the bride"): "'Come!' Let the one who is thirsty come; and let the one who wishes take the free gift of the water of life" (22:17).

▼ Apply

❓ *How has God spoken to you through the words of Revelation?*

❓ *What specific steps are you going to take in response?*

2 PETER: All you need

Throughout church history people have claimed that they've found a secret key to the Christian life that unlocks the door of blessing.

But the message of 2 Peter is: if you trust in Christ, you've already got all that you need.

Read 2 Peter 1:1-4

This letter by Peter, one of the twelve apostles, is a general one, rather than to one specific church.

You've got it!

❷ *How does the faith of the Christians to whom he is writing (and ours today) compare with the faith of the apostles themselves (v 1)?*

❷ *Where has our faith come from?*

❷ *How is Jesus described (v 1-2)? And what blessings do we enjoy through him (v 2)?*

❷ *What do we have by God's power (v 3)? What is the point of the promises God has given us in his word?*

❯ Apply

If you're assembling an IKEA bed and you discover towards the end that a key piece is missing, all your work has been for nothing. But if we trust in Christ, the "package" God has given us contains everything we need.

❷ *Are there times when it doesn't feel like that?*

❷ *When are you (or when have you been) tempted as a Christian to feel that you are missing some key piece of the Christian kit?*

You haven't got it!

It's good to ask not just what a Bible-writer is saying but why he's saying it.

❷ *Why do you think Peter started his letter by encouraging these Christians to remember that in Christ they had all they needed for the Christian life?*

Sometimes the end of a letter gives a clue as to why it was written.

Read 2 Peter 3:17-18

❷ *What was Peter's concern for these Christians?*

❷ *Chapter 2 is all about this threat. Who were these people (2:1)? What were they promising (2:19)?*

❯ Apply

In the Christian world there are always going to be people claiming they have found the secret, and that they have something you haven't got but need. The latest bestseller or craze, a new technique, a new movement—they're attractive, especially to keen Christians who want to grow.

❷ *Can you think of any examples?*

❮ Pray

Pray that God will equip you through this letter to be on your guard and not get carried away. Give thanks that in Christ you have all you need.

Go for it!

Faith is a precious gift from God. But we are not then just to sit back and think, "I believe in Jesus. My sins are forgiven. All sorted. Got my ticket to heaven."

Read 2 Peter 1:5-8

Add

❓ *What must we do instead (v 5)?*

Verse 5 begins "For this very reason..."

❓ *What reasons are there in verses 3-4 for doing this?*

Put into your own words what each quality in verses 5-7 means:

- Goodness (Note: The same word is used in verse 3 of God himself)

- Knowledge

- Self-control

- Perseverance

- Godliness (Note: contrast those in 2:5 and 3: 7)

- Mutual affection

- Love

This list is not exhaustive. It perhaps picks qualities especially lacking in the false teachers. And it's not a ladder on which you climb from one quality to the next. It's not as if you can only get perseverance once you've got self-control.

⌄ Apply

❓ *How do you measure up to this portrait of Christian character? Where are you stronger, and where are you weaker?*

Like instruments in an orchestra, these qualities together make a beautiful sound.

❓ *What would someone be like if they had a lot of Bible knowledge but little self-control or love? Or heaps of brotherly affection but little knowledge?*

Multiply

❓ *We're not just to be content to have these qualities—what are we to do (1:8a)?*

❓ *What do we need to be doing to grow (v 5)? Put that in your own words.*

Christians have sometimes denied the need for effort. "Victorious life teaching" claimed that the big secret was just to let Christ live through you—"Let go and let God".

❓ *How would you respond to that from this passage?*

⌄ Apply

We should approach life like athletes, always seeking to improve our personal best.

❓ *Is that your mindset? What things could you be doing to grow in knowledge or self-control or love?*

⌃ Pray

Ask God to strengthen you today to make every effort and to not be spiritually lazy.

Worth it

To keep going with anything that requires much effort, we need to be convinced it's worth it. And so with the call to live an increasingly "godly life" (v 3).

Here, Peter gives us the motivation we need.

Motivations for growth
Read 2 Peter 1:8-11

Peter gives four motivations to go for growth.

Motivation One:

❓ *What will growth in the qualities listed in verses 5-7 keep us from (v 8b)?*
❓ *Putting it positively, what will we be like if we do possess these qualities in increasing measure? Why is that motivational?*

Motivation Two:

❓ *If we don't have these qualities, what is that a sign of (v 9)? Why do you think that is?*

Motivation Three:

❓ *What other benefit do we get from going for growth in these qualities (v 10)?*

Our "election" refers to the fact that God chose us to belong to him before we were born or had done anything good. Our life does not secure our election, but it does demonstrate the truth of it.

Motivation Four:

❓ *If we are going for growth, what can we look forward to (v 11)?*

The implication in this verse is that the opposite is also true—that if we don't go for growth, we may just scrape in, or we may end up giving up on the truth and not making it.

⌄ Apply

❓ *How will these four motivations help you in your Christian life? Which of them resonates particularly with you today?*

Need for reminder
Read 2 Peter 1:12-15

This teaching is not new to these Christians (v 12).

❓ *So why is Peter bothering to write to them about it (v 12, 13, 15)?*
❓ *Why is there a sense of urgency for Peter (v 13-15)?*
❓ *How does Peter's perspective on his death link back to verse 11?*

⌃ Pray

Pray that you would take progress in living a godly life as seriously as Peter did; that these motivations would encourage you to make every effort; and that you would not just pursue this yourself, but would also encourage others to, in light of the coming eternal kingdom.

Nothing but the truth

Some dismiss the message about Jesus as a story, or just the opinion of Christians, or as "true for you but not for me". Peter calls two witnesses to prove it is the truth.

Witness One: The New Testament apostles

Read 2 Peter 1:16-18

The "we" in verse 16 is the apostles. The focus of their message was "the coming of our Lord Jesus Christ in power".

Read 2 Peter 1:11; 3:4, 10

❷ *Do you think Peter is referring to Jesus' first or second coming?*

Peter wants to offer evidence to prove this wasn't some story they had made up. He recalls the moment when he and two other disciples walked up a mountain with Jesus.

Read Mark 9:2-10

❷ *Of what were Peter and the other disciples eyewitnesses (2 Peter 1:16b-17a)?*
❷ *Of what were they earwitnesses (v 17b-18)?*
❷ *How does what the apostles saw and heard prove that their teaching about Jesus' promised return was not just a made-up story?*

Witness Two: The Old Testament prophets

Read 2 Peter 1:19-21

The "prophetic message" refers to the whole Old Testament. It is like a light shining in the darkness just before the new day dawns when Jesus returns (i.e. "the morning star rises").

❷ *What should our attitude to it be (v 19)?*
❷ *Where have the OT Scriptures come from and not come from (v 20-21)?*
❷ *What conclusion can we draw about the truthfulness and value of the Bible?*

···· **TIME OUT** ····························

❷ *Read 1 Peter 1:10-11. What two things about Christ did the Old Testament prophets predict?*

That the first has now happened gives us assurance that we will experience the second!

✔ Apply

❷ *How has today's passage strengthened your conviction that Christ really is going to return in power and glory, bringing in the eternal kingdom?*

The Bible is unique—the very words of God.

❷ *Is that reflected in how you treat it? How could your approach to it reflect this more?*

⌃ Pray

Give thanks for the sure testimony of prophecy and history in God's word, and for the certainty we can have that Christ and his kingdom are coming.

Self-destructive tendency

We worry about terrorism, nuclear war, and gun and knife crime. And yet all around us there are millions of people with their thumbs on the self-destruct button.

It's a trap

Read Proverbs 11:3-8

Go through the verses and work out the different ways in which we destroy ourselves.

❷ *Which of these do you think you are most vulnerable to?*

Go on—try it! It will set you free. It is what will lead to your true maturity and independence. This is the lie of Satan, and it has been the same since the Garden of Eden (Genesis 3:1-7). But sin only leads to enslavement (Proverbs 11:6), and to our ultimate ruin. Verse 4 points out that the things we put our trust in—money, wealth and possessions—will be of absolutely no value on the day of judgment, when only one currency will be worth anything: *righteousness.* Likewise, if we put our trust in other people rather than money, that hope too is futile (v 7).

∨ Apply

❷ *How have you seen this truth played out in your own life?*
❷ *How did you find release from the snare of sin?*
❷ *What would be your testimony and advice to another believer who finds themselves "trapped by evil desires" (v 6)?*

City slickers

Read Proverbs 11:9-11

❷ *What aspect of the way we live is brought into focus here?*
❷ *What do you find encouraging in these verses?*

We all live in a wider community, and our words, actions and decisions affect others—even as we ourselves are affected by others. Some Christians have chosen to separate themselves from the world to such an extent that they have little influence and little witness in it. But these verses suggest that Christians can add real value to their communities. When churches or Christians run groups for parents and toddlers or teenagers; or set up food banks; or take part in neighbourhood activities in an open, honest and positive way, these can have an enormous influence for good. It also does a huge amount to show others that Christians are not weird and dangerous, but have love and integrity.

The alternative is that the unrighteous pull others along with them on the road to destruction.

∨ Apply

❷ *Are you and your church cut off from community life, or are you taking part in it to be salt and light? How?*

Watch out!

Many countries publish national threat levels, warning of possible terrorist attacks. In this letter Peter sets the threat level for the church to high.

Why? Because he is writing to warn these Christians of something seriously destructive—false teachers.

Be warned: A profile

Read 2 Peter 2:1-3a

> ❷ *Why does verse 1 begin with the word "but", do you think?*

The false prophets and teachers arise "among the people" and "among you" (v 1).

> ❷ *How does this help us identify who Peter has in mind here? (Hint: Read Acts 20:29-30.)*

With false teaching, there are two extremes to avoid. One is seeing everyone as a false teacher, even when you actually only disagree about secondary issues (that is, things that are important, but not essential for understanding and responding to the gospel). The other is seeing no one as a false teacher and never wanting to draw lines, for fear of causing offence or courting unpopularity.

The false teaching Peter warns about is...

Deceptive (2 Peter 2:1): Jesus warned about wolves in sheep's clothing (Matthew 7:15), which should put us on high alert.

> ❷ *Distorted (2 Peter 2:1, 3): How can we equip ourselves better to spot false teaching?*
> ❷ *Denying (v 1): What do they deny? What do you think this means?*

> ❷ *Destructive (v 1): In what way is false teaching destructive?*

The lives of these false teachers are marked by *depravity* (v 2) and *greed* (v 3a—see also 1 Timothy 6:5).

> ❷ *What effect does this have?*

Such false teachers will be very popular, with many followers (2 Peter 2:2).

> ❷ *Can you think of any examples today, or from your own experience, of the destructiveness of popular false teaching or the exploitation of popular false teachers?*

Be assured: Their fate

Read 2 Peter 2:3b-9

> ❷ *What will be the fate of such false teachers (v 3b)?*

In verses 4-8, Peter gives three historical examples (fallen angels, the flooded world and morally filthy cities) of God condemning the ungodly.

> ❷ *How are these examples applied (v 9)?*

☑ Apply

Read 2 Peter 3:17. This is the reason Peter warns us about these false teachers.

> ❷ *In what way do you need to hear the warning today? Is there anyone you need to pass this warning on to?*

Know your enemy

That Peter devotes a third of his letter to false teachers shows how seriously he took this threat, and how seriously we should too. Here, Peter pictures them as animals...

Wild animals
Read 2 Peter 2:10-16

A pet dog is trained to respect the authority of its master, but a wild tiger is a law unto itself.

❷ *What is the attitude of false teachers to authority (v 10)?*

❷ *How do you think such an attitude to authority might show itself in the way false teachers...*
  • *handle the Bible?* • *view themselves?*

And like wild animals, the false teachers don't exercise self-control but instead act on instinct.

❷ *What is the problem with their eyes and heart (v 14)?*

❷ *What other verses speak of their sexual immorality and financial greed?*

❷ *How will their fate be like that of animals (v 12)?*

False teachers may be highly intelligent, but in the end they are more dimwitted than donkeys (v 16). The reference is to an incident when the prophet Balaam was rebuked by his own donkey, who had more spiritual sense than he did (Numbers 22:21-31)!

Ruthless fishermen
Read 2 Peter 2:17-19

The word "entice" (v 18, or "seduce" in v 14) is a fishing image. It's used of fishermen

luring fish with bait that disguises the hook.

❷ *What is the bait the false teachers use to catch people (v 18-19)?*

❷ *What kind of things do you imagine them saying?*

They prey on the vulnerable—young Christians, the spiritually immature or those who are struggling (v 14, 18).

Filthy pigs and dogs
Read 2 Peter 2:20-22

It's not clear whether this describes the false teachers alone or their victims as well.

❷ *What is so tragic about these people (v 20-21)?*

❷ *In what way are they like pigs and dogs (v 22)?*

▾ Apply

The take-home from this is very simple and straightforward (3:17).

❷ *How should this warning about false teachers shape...*
  • *how you listen to Bible teaching (either spoken or written)?*
  • *how you decide what church to join when you move to a new area?*
  • *how you choose people for leadership positions in church?*

Pray for protection from false teaching for your own church family and leaders.

Remember, remember

In the Bible's final chapter, Jesus says three times that he is coming soon. The personal, literal return of Jesus, bringing the end of this world, fills the New Testament horizon...

... but it might not always fill ours—which is why we need today's passage.

Read 2 Peter 3:1-9

Necessary reminder

> ❷ *Why did Peter write this letter (v 1-2, see also 1:12)?*
> ❷ *In the light of 3:4, what particular "words" of the prophets and "command" of the Lord through the apostles does Peter seem to have in mind? (Hint: Read Malachi 4:1 and Matthew 24:36.)*

The word for "stimulate" (2 Peter 3:1) is used elsewhere of waking up someone who is sleeping (see Luke 8:24). There is a danger that we get spiritually sleepy. The biblical teaching about the Lord's return is designed to wake us up (see Matthew 24:42).

Sinful scoffing

The "last days" are the time between Christ's first coming and his return.

> ❷ *What will scoffers say (2 Peter 3:3-4)? What reason will they give?*
> ❷ *In what way do you think "evil desires" might be linked to dismissing the Lord's return?*

We expect non-Christians to dismiss the idea of the Lord returning in judgment, but the warning here is about false teachers and leaders in the church doing the same.

Certain word

> ❷ *In verses 5-7, what evidence that God's word (which says the Lord will return) is to be trusted does Peter point to?*
> ❷ *What does that same word promise about the future?*

Merciful delay

It's now been 2,000 years since Jesus said he would return soon.

> ❷ *Why should that not worry us (v 8-9; see also Psalm 90:4)?*
> ❷ *What is the reason for the delay?*

⌄ Apply

> ❷ *When do you find it hardest to believe that the Lord really will return?*
> ❷ *How has this passage strengthened your assurance that he will?*

⌃ Pray

Give thanks for this reminder and wake-up call from God. Give thanks that the Lord didn't return the day before you repented and believed the gospel. Pray you will keep living a life of obedient faith, and making the most of gospel opportunities.

The end is nigh, so…

It has been said that humans can live about 40 days without food, about three days without water and about eight minutes without air… but only a second without hope.

We were reminded in 2 Peter 3:1-9 that the Lord is going to return. Today's passage unpacks what will happen on that "day of the Lord", and how should it shape our lives today.

Read 2 Peter 3:10-14

Future

❷ *In what sense do you think "the day of the Lord will come like a thief" (see also Matthew 24:44)?*
❷ *What will happen to this present world on that day (2 Peter 3:10-12)?*
❷ *Why is that day nevertheless one filled with hope for God's people (v 13; see also Isaiah 65:17; Matthew 19:28; Revelation 21:1)?*

This is not like counting down to Christmas or a significant birthday. There will be no countdown…

···· TIME OUT ·································

The language of destruction in these verses might lead us to conclude that nothing is going to be left of this present creation, and that God will create a brand new universe from scratch. But the same kind of language is used elsewhere of our physical bodies, which are in fact going to be redeemed, raised and transformed. In the same way, it seems that this present world will emerge from the coming destruction redeemed and transformed. **Read Romans 8:19-23.**

Present

❷ *Given what will happen on the day of God, what should be our attitude to that day in the present (2 Peter 3:12-14)?*
❷ *How should looking forward to the day of God shape the way that we live now (v 11, 14)? Why (v 13)?*

✓ Apply

We might expect the main application of knowing that the day of the Lord is coming to be: *warn non-Christians and tell them the gospel.* But instead Peter here sees it as a motivation for us to keep making every effort to live holy and godly lives (which, of course, includes but is not summed up by evangelism). Such living is an indispensable mark of people heading for life in the new creation, "where righteousness dwells", in contrast to those heading for the "destruction of the ungodly" (v 7).

❷ *How does your view of your life, your hopes and the world around you today need to be shaped by this passage? (Make sure you're being specific in your answer.)*

⌃ Pray

Pray that you would be looking forward to this future more and more—and that it would motivate you to live "holy and godly lives" in the present more and more.

Holding and growing

To "coast" means "to move without power or with as little effort as possible". The Christian who is coasting is in the danger zone, and needs to step on the gas.

Hold on to the word
Read 2 Peter 3:15-16

> ❷ How does the message of Paul's letters compare to Peter's message in this one? Why is Peter highlighting this, do you think?
> ❷ What is the significance of the phrase "the other Scriptures"? How does verse 15 confirm this view of Paul's writings?

The need to be godly in the light of the Lord's return is the united testimony of God's word. It's something we need to take seriously. But it's a truth that is under attack.

In his letters Paul wrote "with the wisdom that God gave him," says Peter.

> ❷ But how do some people treat what he wrote?
> ❷ What different fates do these two different attitudes to Scripture lead to (v 15-16)?

⌄ Apply

False teachers will quote the Bible but twist and distort what it says. It's the same satanic strategy used by the serpent in the Garden of Eden, and by the devil tempting Jesus in the wilderness. We need to be on guard.

> ❷ For example: to justify ungodliness or avoid disapproval from the culture, how might someone distort the truth that we are saved by grace alone through faith,

and not by good works? Or the truth that God is love?

Grow in the grace
Read 2 Peter 3:17-18

> ❷ What danger are we warned about here?
> ❷ How can we make sure this doesn't happen to us (v 18)?

Peter's readers were "firmly established in the truth" (1:12). If they needed this warning not to lose their stability, we all do. The term "fall" (3:17) is used in Galatians 5:4 of falling away from grace, and in Acts 27:26 and 29 of a ship running aground and being shipwrecked. Beware of shipwrecking your faith!

⌄ Apply

Spiritual health and stability are not just about guarding against error—we need to secure our faith, display the truth of our election, and grow healthily.

> ❷ What are you doing to grow in the grace and knowledge of the Lord? Are there other things you should be doing?
> ❷ As we finish our time in 2 Peter, how would you summarise its message if a Christian friend asked you about it?
> ❷ And how would you summarise the way it has encouraged you?

Bible in a year: Jeremiah 6-8 • Matthew 21 v 23-46

1 TIMOTHY: The secret

Who wrote this letter, and to whom? Why did he write—what is it all about? The first question is answered in the opening verses—the second question later in the letter.

Who?

Read 1 Timothy 1:1-2

The letter opens, as was common, by describing the sender and the recipient.

- ❓ *Who wrote it, and how does he describe himself (v 1)?*
- ❓ *Who received it, and how does the writer describe their relationship (v 2)?*
- ❓ *How should this affect how we read the letter, do you think?*

An apostle was somebody who was sent on a mission—something like an ambassador. This was by divine appointment, not self-selection—read 2:7. But if Timothy is Paul's "son in the faith" (1:2), why does Paul need to underline that he (Paul) is, truthfully, a God-appointed apostle? The best explanation is that this letter was not a private correspondence but intended to be a public letter of recommendation for Timothy—something like us giving a reference for someone to a potential new employer.

Why?

Read 1 Timothy 3:14-16

- ❓ *In Paul's physical absence, what will this letter enable Timothy to know (v 14-15)?*
- ❓ *What will spring from knowing the "mystery" of which Paul speaks in v 16?*

Paul is writing to this man of God to tell him how to conduct himself among the people of God. It is not about how he may *like* to conduct himself, but how he *must* conduct himself among God's household.

3:16 is the most important verse in the letter, but it causes many a reader to scratch their head. "Mystery" is a key word for Paul, but it is not a helpful translation because it does not really mean "mystery"! Paul is not speaking of something impossible to understand, or deeply spiritual, or irrational. Paul means "secret": something that was once hidden and has now been made public. For example, I may choose to hide my birthday from you. So it becomes a secret, unless and until I reveal it to you.

As we relate to the one true God and Father of our Lord Jesus Christ, we pursue right behaviour—but that is not what "godliness" is. "Godliness" is about relating to your god rightly. The great secret of godliness is found not in our approach to God but in his approach to us. It is not in our moral or religious activities, but in God's gospel of his Son, who appeared in the flesh, was vindicated by the Spirit, seen by angels, preached among the nations, believed on in the world and taken up in glory.

🔼 Pray

Pray that, as you read this letter, you would come to more fully understand and appreciate how God has come to you in Jesus, and that this would shape the way you live in response to that.

Three types of talk

"Sticks and stones may break my bones but words will never hurt me." How wrong can a proverb be? Today we look at three kinds of words that harm or heal.

Keep quiet
Read Proverbs 11:12

❓ *What situation is pictured in this verse?*
❓ *Bring to mind some occasions when you have experienced the first half of the verse. How did it feel? What did you do?*
❓ *Why do you think the writer believes this sort of person "has no sense"?*
❓ *What is the wise thing to do instead?*

Mocking someone who lives in close community with you is bound to be destructive to your relationship. There's a high probability that it will rebound on you in some way. Instead, the sensible thing is to keep quiet. Naming someone's shortcomings or giving rein to our bad opinion of them is unloving; and we are called to *love* our neighbours as ourselves, not insult them before others.

✔ Apply

❓ *When are you tempted to do this?*
❓ *How can you train yourself to speak positively and kindly of others?*
❓ *How might you be able to change a conversation that is critical of someone into one that is more wholesome?*

Keep quieter
Read Proverbs 11:13

❓ *What kinds of people are contrasted here?*

❓ *Why is gossip so destructive?*
❓ *Think of the people you know. Who would you trust to share a secret with? Who would you not trust?*
❓ *Why might people pass on secrets?*

When someone confides in us, they are opening themselves up at the very deepest level. When we pass their secret on, it may be because we want to look good before others by sharing a "juicy secret", or because we want to invite others to judge them with us. Whatever the reason, to pass on a secret is to betray someone at a fundamental level and will be deeply wounding for them and for your relationship with them. As perpetrator, we need to repent of such gossip; or as victim, we need to pick carefully who we share with.

Taking counsel
Read Proverbs 11:14

❓ *What is at stake in this proverb?*
❓ *What are we being encouraged to do?*
❓ *Do you think this is applicable on a personal level as well as a national one?*

There are times, of course, when seeking advice from many people is just our way of looking around for someone to agree with our already-decided course of action. But for the most part, it is true that the more we access the wise advice of others, the more likely we are to make good decisions.

❓ *What do you need to seek advice on?*

Truth matters

Our world is in love with love. And sometimes our message of love melds easily with the world's love. Yet, to our world, Paul's charge in 1:3 sounds anything but loving...

Read 1 Timothy 1:3-7

❷ *What does Paul want Timothy to command particular people (v 3-4a)?*
❷ *What is the goal in commanding these people to stop (v 5)?*

But... where's the love in Paul telling Timothy to impose his view and what he thinks on another, in opposition to their view and what they think? Surely we have moved beyond somebody charging others to be silent.

❷ *But why is it so important that Timothy commands these people to stop teaching (v 4, 6-7)?*

These false teachers have swerved from the foundational motivation of Paul and Timothy—from the gospel. And, having deviated from this, they have turned towards vain or empty and meaningless discussions. Theirs was not an immediate denial of the gospel but a departure from its spiritual effects that led on to the emptiness of falsehood. The result is ignorant and arrogant teachers, who want to be teachers of the law but do not know what they are talking about (v 7).

···· TIME OUT ····

❷ *Have you witnessed or experienced teachers like this within the church?*
❷ *What damaging effects did they have on the gospel faith of others?*
❷ *How popular were they?*

The central problem with this false teaching is that it does not promote the "stewardship" (v 4, ESV) from God. The stewardship of God is God's plan of salvation—his plan and management. The whole programme of God is not about speculative myths and genealogies—it is not an intellectual game to be played. God's programme is about salvation by faith and restored relationship with himself. God's plan is fulfilled in a man who said he was *"the* way *the* truth·and *the* life"* (John 14:6, emphasis added).

Truth is found and taught not simply in affirmations but also in rebuttals. When errors are opposed, it highlights both the details and the importance of the truth. Yet to oppose errors and those who teach them requires not only a firm grasp of the truth but also the emotional strength to keep standing firm. Charging false teachers to desist from their teaching is not consistent with this world's version of love, but it does flow necessarily from Christ's love for his church.

⌃ Pray

Thank God for the truth he has revealed in his Son, the Lord Jesus. Thank God for his flawless word, all about his Son. Thank God for those who teach you his gospel from his word, and equip you to spot and counter error, rather than falling for it. Pray that they would continue to have the conviction and emotional energy to stand courageously.

Bible in a year: Jeremiah 15-17 • Matthew 23 v 1-22

Law, gospel, and us

Understanding the role of the Old Testament law in Christian life has been an abiding problem. The gospel brings liberty, but we struggle not to live in legalism or licence.

Read 1 Timothy 1:8-11

Paul's instruction to Timothy here is not the sum total of what he says about the law, but it is a very important part of the New Testament teaching about God's law.

The law in 1 Timothy

- ❷ *What does Paul affirm (v 8)? What condition ("if...") does he attach?*
- ❷ *Who is the law "for" (v 9-11)? What do you understand Paul to mean by this?*
- ❷ *What does Paul say about the gospel (v 11)?*

The law in the OT

God gave the law to Israel with great fanfare at Mount Sinai. While the people of Israel were willing to enter into covenant with God, they didn't really want to hear what he had to say. Their fearful and rebellious hearts kept them from embracing God's law—and their subsequent history demonstrated a remarkable resistance to it. The promise of the new covenant is not so much of a new law, but rather a new heart that is able to receive the law—**read Jeremiah 31:31-34.**

So who is the law for?

People who are "righteous" (1 Timothy 1:9) do not need the law to condemn them or constrain them. They do what is right. So,

Paul says, the law is given for people who are not right—in particular the "lawbreakers", who live out their lawlessness in immorality.

So do Christians, justified by God's grace, now still need the Old Testament law? Yes—first, because through our Lord Jesus Christ, this is the law that is written on our hearts by the Spirit, who moves us to obey it as we hear it. And second, because while we live in this world, our sinful desires of lawlessness keep waging war with the Spirit.

Notice that Paul says that the lawless deeds of verses 9-10 are contrary to the sound doctrine that conforms to the gospel (v 11). The things the law opposes are the very things the gospel also opposes. The very reason the law had to be given is not ignored by the gospel, but rather addressed in the gospel. To set the law against the gospel is a great mistake. The law drives us to the gospel, and the gospel moves us to obey the law.

✔ Apply

- ❷ *Are you more tempted to live in legalism (obeying God's law to earn/keep his favour) or in licence (disobeying God's law because you are right with him by grace)? In what ways?*
- ❷ *How does Paul's teaching about the law here help you to obey it out of a gospel motivation? What will change in your behaviour as you do this?*

He came to save you

Have you ever considered how surprising, and kind, it is that God has not only saved you through faith in his Son, but also gives you work to do in proclaiming his Son?

Paul had. He never grew less than awe-struck about it.

Grace for a blasphemer

Read 1 Timothy 1:12-14

❷ *What is Paul grateful for (v 12)?*
❷ *Why is this particularly amazing (v 13)?*

To modern ears, blasphemy is not such a great crime. But in God's world, blasphemy is so serious as to be the one unforgivable sin (Mark 3:28-30). We have reduced "blasphemy" to swearing—vulgar, meaningless references to God. But Paul's blasphemy was much more than that. His was the intentional opposition to Jesus seen in his murderous persecution of Christians. He set out to destroy Jesus' messianic claim by persecuting his followers.

What does it mean that Paul received mercy "because I acted in ignorance and unbelief" (v 13)? Does that mean ignorant unbelief is excusable? In the Law of Moses, God differentiates between sins that are unintentional and those which express defiance—"sinning with a high hand", as it is called (e.g. Numbers 15:27-31). Saul of Tarsus was forgiven his blasphemy because it was the unintentional sin of ignorance and unbelief. He needed salvation in the same way that a lost sheep, straying by its own stupidity, culpable yet helpless, needs rescue. He didn't intend to blaspheme the Lord—just the reverse: he thought he was honouring him.

A trustworthy saying

Read 1 Timothy 1:15-17

❷ *How does Paul describe the work of Jesus (v 15)?*
❷ *How does Paul define himself (v 15)?*
❷ *How would this view of himself enable him to more fully appreciate all that Jesus came to do for sinners?*

Notice what Paul says Christ displayed in saving him. He could have rightly said "mercy", "kindness" or "power"—but he writes "immense patience" (v 16). God is immensely patient. He is slow to anger, and in his slowness he endures the ongoing sinfulness of people. He could have rightly finished the world the day Adam ate the fruit. He could have killed Saul when he zealously took part in killing Christ's servant Stephen (Acts 7:58; 8:1). But he had other plans for the world, and for Saul. Christ's "immense patience" with Paul gives hope to all who are still alive—there is still time to believe in him for eternal life.

❷ *What does Paul's view of himself and of Christ move him to do (v 17)?*

⌃ Pray

Consider your own sinfulness, and the truth that "Christ Jesus came into the world to save sinners"—even Paul, and even you.

Then use verses 12 and 17 to praise and thank your Saviour.

Bible in a year: Jeremiah 20-21 • Matthew 24 v 1-28

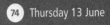
First of all...

Paul is entrusting his gospel ministry to Timothy. This passage shows us that the stakes could not be higher—and where Timothy should begin with this weighty charge.

High stakes

Read 1 Timothy 1:18-20

> ❷ *What is "this command" (v 18—look back to v 3-4)?*
> ❷ *Why does it matter so much that Timothy does this (v 19-20)?*

Paul's aim in handing these men over to Satan is that they may learn not to blaspheme. Paul had been a blasphemer—though he acted in ignorance and unbelief (v 13). This pair are apparently becoming blasphemers in knowledge and defiance. They are therefore in greater danger of going beyond forgiveness (Mark 3:28-30).

Our first recourse

Read 1 Timothy 2:1-4

> ❷ *What does Paul urge Timothy to do "first of all" (v 1)?*

It is not clear how this command relates to the problem of false teaching and wandering from the faith that Timothy is to address. But we should not miss the simple point: when faced with any challenge or command, our first recourse should be to prayer.

☑ Apply

> ❷ *What are you in the habit of praying about, and why?*

What to pray for

> ❷ *What does Timothy to pray for (v 1-2)?*
> ❷ *Why (v 2)?*

God appoints governments as his servants for our good (Romans 13:1-7). The decisions of these powerful people can facilitate or frustrate the ability of others to lead the kind of life that pleases God (1 Timothy 2:3). So we are to pray for those in high position, that they might enable us to live a good life that pleases God. Our rulers' decisions about work hours, weekends, justice, marriage laws, censorship or any other matter affect the way we live, making it easier or harder to live a God-pleasing life (a life based on the secret of godliness, 3:14-16).

> ❷ *What does God desire (v 3-4)?*
> ❷ *So if we are blessed with the ability to "live peaceful and quiet lives", how would God like us to use them, do you think?*

☑ Apply

> ❷ *How much freedom do your "rulers" (your government, your boss at work, and so on) allow you to worship Christ in how you live, and proclaim Christ in how you speak?*
> ❷ *How are you going to use your freedom to do these things?*

Finish this study on prayer by spending time praying...

One God, one mediator

If Christians are free to live godly lives, then God is pleased—because living in godliness means speaking the gospel, and proclaiming the truth is how people are saved.

What God wants
Read 1 Timothy 2:3-4

Like a lifeguard or lifesaver at the pool or the beach, God desires to save whoever needs saving.

> ❷ *What do people need to know in order to be saved (v 4)?*

The great truth
Read 1 Timothy 2:5-7

> ❷ *What is "the truth" that people need to know to be saved (v 5-6)?*
> ❷ *How does this truth mean that the gospel is both completely inclusive and totally exclusive?*

This is the great statement of monotheism: "For [or "because"] there is one God" (v 5). The logic of there being only one God is that there is only one God for all of humanity to worship and serve. And there is also only one God who can save us; and he has done so by coming in the person of Jesus to become our mediator. A mediator is someone who brings about reconciliation between two parties who are otherwise in disagreement or at war. That mediator will need to enjoy the confidence of both parties to persuade them to settle their accounts and make peace. Humans may want any number of mediators, but the only one acceptable to God is his Son. He became human ("the man Christ Jesus") in order

to be able to represent God to us and us to God.

We are the offending party, and God is the one offended against. The method of Christ's mediatory work is spelled out in verse 6: he "gave himself as a ransom for all". Jesus himself described his sacrificial death as giving a ransom (Matthew 20:28; Mark 10:45), on behalf of and as a substitute for others. This ransoming death of Jesus is the testimony—the witness to and argument for—the character of God the Saviour, who desires all people to be saved.

The gospel of Jesus is not offered to a single nation or a particular people group. It is the announcement that the one God over all humanity does not desire the death of any sinner, but that each would turn and live (Ezekiel 18:23, 32)—and that in Christ's mediatory, ransoming death any and every man and woman, whatever their position in society or on earth, may be saved.

> ❷ *What is Paul's role in the great plan of "God our Saviour" (1 Timothy 2:7)?*

⌄ Apply

We are not called to be apostles, but we are called to be heralds.

> ❷ *God wants all people to be saved. Do you want all people around you to be saved?*
> ❷ *What are you doing to tell them of the one God and one mediator?*

Men and women

*These verses speak into a controversy that has divided Christian thinking for a gener-
ation. We should be wary of our own natural bias towards one direction or another.*

A word to men

Read 1 Timothy 2:8

❷ *What does Paul want men to do?*
❷ *What must they avoid as they do this?*
❷ *Why might men need to be told both the
positive and the negative here, do you
think?*

The key is not the physical posture of
hand-lifting. In the Bible many different
and mutually exclusive postures of prayer
are described. The essential posture is that
of the contrite and humble heart, and a
peaceful outlook. Anger and fighting are, in
most senses, the opposite of prayer.

A word to women

Read 1 Timothy 2:9-15

❷ *What is your instinctive reaction to these
verses? Why?*

Paul raises two issues: apparel and learning.

❷ *What does he say about women's
clothes?*

Paul is calling upon women to think for
themselves about how they adorn themselves so that they can present themselves
in a way that is consistent with their
Christian faith. His examples of immodest
dressing are just illustrations. We must not
become legalistic, as if women must never
braid their hair or wear a gold ring or a
pearl necklace.

❷ *What does he say about how women
learn from the Scriptures (v 11-12)?*

"Quiet" can refer to silence, but equally it
can refer to a quiet demeanour (see 1 Peter
3:4). That appears to be the sense here.

❷ *What two reasons does Paul give for his
commands here (1 Timothy 2:13-14)?*

God's order of creation (v 13) is significant
in the Bible's understanding of authority.
God gave the role of leadership to Adam.
Men and women are equal, but they are not
the same. And in the fall, God judged the
man for following his wife's leading rather
than stepping up to lead himself (Genesis
3:17). Eve was deceived, but Adam was not
deceived—he had directly received God's
command (2:16-17). He wilfully, knowingly
became a sinner.

1 Timothy 2:15 is confusing (and space is
short!): suffice it to say that it is not saying
that every woman must have children,
nor that every woman who has children
is saved, but that the work of the gospel
restores the order of creation.

✔ Apply

❷ *What will it look like for you, as a man
or a woman, to live out these verses
faithfully and wisely?*
❷ *Are there aspects of these verses that you
need to pray or think about or discuss
more fully? How will you do so?*

Contradictions?

"The Bible is full of contradictions," some say. How can you possibly believe it? But our experience of life is also full of contradictions—and these are reflected in these verses.

Confused?

Read Proverbs 11:15

❷ *How do you respond to this verse? What is it that feels wrong about it?*

❷ *What aspect of this is simply true to life?*

❷ *Do you think there's an unchristian way that this verse could be (mis)applied?*

There's a big difference between naivety and innocence—and that distinction is at the heart of this saying. Of course God loves generosity, and of course Christians are called to give to others without worrying if they will be paid back. But we are also called to give *intelligently*. We should not give to and support those who will not work, for example (2 Thessalonians 3:6-10).

We could use this proverb as an excuse to not give to or fund anyone at all. Or we could use it as a warning to be careful and selective in how we deploy our resources for greatest effect, and to be wary of committing ourselves. In the context of the Bible's call to generosity, this proverb is not contradicting that call—it should be seen as one piece of advice in the context of the bigger picture.

Read Proverbs 11:16-18

❷ *To what attitudes and character traits is money linked in these verses?*

❷ *What should Christians be more concerned about than gaining wealth?*

Our culture places huge value on wealth, but here it is seen as insignificant when compared with honour. Its value is "deceptive (v 18), so the godly look for a "sure reward" that is given by God to those who work at righteousness. Kindness (v 16) and righteousness (v 18) are what we should set our aims on daily. Some self-help books tell us that to be successful, we should fix our gaze on ruthlessly pursuing profit, or focus on what makes us feel good. But God tells us to resolutely pursue goodness towards others.

···· **TIME OUT** ··

Read Matthew 6:19-34

❷ *What do you find most challenging about these verses?*

⌃ Pray

Ask the Lord to give you opportunities to show kindness to others today. Pray for the wisdom to know when to give to others, and when to lovingly withhold support.

Have you joined the *Explore* Facebook Group yet?

Ask your questions, engage with *Explore* editors and writers, and share your thoughts and prayer requests with others who read the Bible with *Explore* day by day. Join today.

www.facebook.com/groups/tgbc.explore

A noble thing

Next, Paul sets out the qualifications for taking on something "noble". But what is this noble thing, and who should undertake it?

Read 1 Timothy 3:1-7

What the task is

❓ *What aspiration does Paul have in mind (v 1)?*

❓ *What difference does it make that Paul says this is a noble task rather than "role", "job" or "office", do you think?*

Each denomination has their particular pattern of ministry and ministers, and each uses this passage to give titles and names to their leaders. So different denominations use the same name to refer to ministries that are different in their appointment, responsibilities and activities (e.g. bishops, priests, and deacons, or elders and teaching elders, or pastors and deacons). It helps to note that the thing Paul says is noble to aspire to is not a position but a task.

❓ *What is the task (end of v 5)?*

To "manage"and "take care of" has the sense of being in charge and caring for. This is indeed a noble task, for the church is a "pillar and buttress of the truth" (v 15).

The qualities required

The character of the men who give leadership in God's household is critically important to the health of the church. In a sense, Paul's list of qualities in v 2-5 should be growing in all Christian men. Nearly all are about character rather than competencies.

❓ *For each, what would this quality look like in daily life in your particular culture and church?*

❓ *What limitations does Paul add (v 6-7)?*

First, worldly leadership is about significance, importance and power. Christian leadership is about service and caring, sacrificial love. A recent convert may not yet see the difference and, imbued with worldly thinking, fall prey to pride. Second, if an overseer has given outsiders no reason to think well of him, or (worse) every reason to think poorly of him, he may well fall into such disgrace that he has been trapped by the devil and is brought down.

⌄ Apply

❓ *Men: to what extent are these characteristics descriptive of you? Where can you be encouraged? How do you need to change?*

❓ *Women: to what extent are these characteristics the ones you most admire in men? (Of course, many of them are equally to be pursued by women.)*

⌃ Pray

Pray for the overseers in your church: that these characteristics would more and more describe them, that God would protect them from serious failure in these areas, and that they would manage your church faithfully.

In the same way…

From one noble task, Paul turns to another—that of the deacon. But again, we have to ask: What is a deacon, and who should undertake this task?

What is a deacon?

Among the problems of translating this word into modern English as "deacon" is the different meaning that various ecclesiastical traditions give to the word.

Read 1 Timothy 4:6

The word translated as "servant" (ESV) or (less helpfully!) "minister" (NIV) here is translated "deacon" in 3:8.

❓ *What difference does that make to our understanding of what a deacon might be?*

It would be better in 3:8-13 to translate the word in the usual way as "servant" and work out from the passage what Paul was talking about.

In this sense, then, these verses speak to all of us, for all of us are called to be servants of the greatest of all Servants. We are never more like Jesus than when we serve others well (Mark 10:42-45; Philippians 2:5-11).

What is a deacon like?

Read 1 Timothy 3:8-13

❓ *What are the similarities between the character required to be an overseer (v 1-7) and a deacon here?*
❓ *What are the differences?*

Verse 11 could be referring to women who are deacons/servants (as the NIV suggests)

or to the wives of men who are deacons/ servants (as the ESV renders it). The Greek is unclear, but the point is: whether we think of servants' wives or female servants, their character and behaviour is to be the same as that of the male "servants".

Any attempt to be precise about the work of the servants is still as doomed to failure as any precise description of the work of the overseer. Timothy is being told how one ought to behave in the household of God. The keys to that behaviour are what we would call morality and ethics, not performance and task. Being a deacon or overseer are activities to be sought and prized, rather than offices to be pursued or wielded. The person who has the characteristics described here for deacons will be someone who serves humbly, wisely and helpfully in God's household.

⌄ Apply

Think about your attitude towards, commitment to and activity within your own local church.

❓ *Would other church members describe you as a "servant"? Why/why not?*

As you did in yesterday's study, check through this list of characteristics.

❓ *Which do you need to grow in? About which can you give thanks that the Spirit has already been growing you in?*

Godliness and gratitude

A modern guide to godliness might be called "The Six Steps of Godliness" and contain a list of things to do. But Paul gives a list of six things God has already done in Jesus.

Godliness revealed

Read 1 Timothy 3:14-16

3:14-16 is the centre-point of 1 Timothy, and it is the centre of Paul's argument and gives the reason for him writing. It reveals the "mystery" (or better "secret") of godliness— what God has done for us. So, godliness requires no rules to keep, no steps to follow, no habits to form, no activities to engage in, no clubs to join and no fees to pay, and there are no key performance indicators to achieve. Godliness is not about us but about God. (The NIV translation of v 16a is unhelpful; the ESV translates it far better, simply as "Great indeed, we confess, is the mystery of godliness...")

❷ *What six things has God done in Jesus (v 16)?*

The first of these is usually understood to refer to the incarnation, when God became flesh. But it is much more likely to refer to Jesus' bodily resurrection, when he appeared (was manifested) repeatedly to the disciples.

In the first century, and for a Jewish man like Paul, the idea that the Jewish Messiah would be "believed on in the world" was wonderful and slightly extraordinary. But that is what Paul was seeing all around him—as the gospel went out to the nations, all manner of people were coming to faith in Jesus.

❷ *What will knowing the "mystery of godliness" (the gospel) allow Timothy, and all Christians, to know (v 15)?*

TIME OUT

❷ *What goes wrong when professing Christians get these two—believing the gospel and conducting yourself rightly— the other way round to how Paul does?*

Gratitude for creation

Read 1 Timothy 4:1-5

❷ *What problem does Paul introduce in verses 1-2?*

This is a harsh description, but it is mild compared to the damage these people do to others (2 Timothy 2:17-18).

❷ *What are these false teachers saying (1 Timothy 4:3)?*
❷ *What is the error in this (v 4-5)?*

Ascetics say the world is evil; materialists say tit is accidental—neither worldview sees it as good, nor do they give humans spiritual responsibility for it. The Bible does.

⌄ Apply

❷ *How do verses 4-5 show us how to enjoy good things in this creation without worshipping them?*
❷ *How can you make sure that you are receiving "with thanksgiving" the good things that God has given you?*

Hard training

The truth matters, and it is eternally wonderful. And so false teaching matters, and it is infinitely damaging. Therefore Timothy's ministry is going to be hard work...

Read 1 Timothy 4:6-10

Point it out

❓ *What are the "things" Timothy must point out to the church (v 1-5)?*

Timothy is not to remain silent about error and falsehood but to expose error by teaching the truth: "the truths of the faith and of the good teaching that you have followed" (v 6).

Labour and strive

❓ *What is Timothy not to do, and what is he to do (v 7)?*

❓ *What is the main point Paul wants to make in verse 8, do you think? (Hint: it is not about the benefits of physical exercise!)*

The metaphor here carries with it the sense of hard, persistent and repetitive work. Those who depart from the faith are "devoting themselves" to deceitful spirits and teachings of demons (v 1, ESV)), just as the false teachers "devote themselves" to myths and endless genealogies in 1:4. Now Timothy is directed to train himself in accordance with or relation to godliness. This is not a command to practise Christian behaviour, but to commit himself to the gospel and its teaching, in contrast to pagan and silly myths. Training in this message is beneficial in ways that surpass the benefits of physical training.

There is not universal agreement as to whether the "trustworthy saying" mentioned in 4:9 is referring to the whole or parts of the preceding verse 8 or the following verse 10. Both sayings point to the salvation that is in Christ Jesus by the gospel message—the great confession of the secret of godliness.

The word "believe" (v 10) does not refer to an intellectual understanding (though that is part of it) but to trust. Trusting God, particularly trusting Jesus, God's only Son, and his death for us is the only way to receive salvation. Hope in the living God, who is the Saviour of all people, is an expression of such trust. So this verse is not teaching that all are saved.

❓ *What do the truths of verses 8 and 9 prompt Paul to do with his life (v 10)?*

The word "labour" is one of hard, wearying work; "strive" is a word meaning fighting and struggling.

❓ *What is this showing Timothy (and us) about Christian ministry?*

⌄ Apply

❓ *Are you willing to listen to your church leader when they decide to point out falsehood in order to safeguard truth?*

❓ *Pastoring the household of God requires labouring and striving. How can you encourage your church's leaders today to keep going in their work?*

A diligent young pastor

Timothy's ministry is to have all the confidence of somebody who knows and teaches the truth of the gospel.

Commanded
Read 1 Timothy 4:11-12

❓ *What is Timothy to do with "these things"—all that Paul has told Timothy about discipleship so far (v 11)?*

Within the church Timothy is to *command* behaviour that befits the household of God.

☑ Apply

❓ *Are you willing to hear a command from the pulpit, based on God's word, to behave in a particular way?*

Problems with youth

In commanding anybody to do anything, there are times when we meet resistance.

❓ *What might be a particular reason for resistance to Timothy (v 12)?*
❓ *What is he to do about it (v 12)?*

In the Bible, the older tends to lead the younger. The idea of the younger leading or having any authority over the older is so rare as to be noticed as being unnatural (e.g. Genesis 25:23; John 1:15; Romans 9:12).

Paul's point in verse 12 is that Timothy can't stop someone thinking negatively about him, but he can remove any reason for it— and he can even provide, in speech and conduct, reason for them to think of him positively.

Encouragement
Read 1 Timothy 4:13-16

❓ *What else does Paul tell him to do?*
• *v 13*   • *v 14*   • *v 15*   • *v 16a*
❓ *What is the motivation for persevering in all this (v 16b)?*

The word "public" in "public reading" is not in the Greek of verse 13—it is assumed from two words that follow: "preaching" ("exhortation", ESV) and "teaching". **Read Acts 13:15 and 15:31**. Both times, the word of exhortation involves teaching people the meaning of the Bible. So Paul is telling Timothy to bring the encouragement of the Scriptures to the people, reading about and then teaching them of the great secret of godliness.

In 1 Timothy 4:14 Paul is taking Timothy back to the clear prophecy concerning the gift that God had given him, in order to encourage him to keep going, undaunted by opponents or those who look down on him.

☑ Apply

❓ *If you are in gospel ministry of some kind, how do these verses encourage you?*
❓ *If you are a church member who listens to the teaching of a younger person, are you in any danger of looking down on them in some way? How can you listen to and think of them in a way that helps you grow, and encourages them?*

Family values

We are not to treat those in our church as customers, nor even as citizens or neighbours. We are to relate to them as relatives—members of the same loving family.

Older and younger
Read 1 Timothy 5:1-2

❓ *Which relationships within the church does Paul have in view here?*

❓ *Imagine Timothy did the opposite of what Paul commands here. What problems would this cause?*

When it comes to older men and women, Paul is effectively saying, *As you would/ should honour your father and mother, so speak words of encouragement to these older saints.* When it comes to younger men and women, Timothy needs to treat them as equals, and not look down on them.

When it comes to his relationships with women younger than him, there is a difference that Timothy must remember—sexual drive (which is itself a good, created thing, but of course is so often used sinfully). Sinful men have a particular need for warning to behave "with absolute purity".

⌄ Apply

Compare the way you think of, pray for and speak to older men and women, and younger people (especially those of the opposite sex) with the way Paul sets out here.

❓ *Is there anything you need to repent of (and perhaps seek forgiveness for)?*

❓ *How can you positively contribute to the strengthening of the family that your church is?*

Caring for widows
Read 1 Timothy 5:3-16

Paul now turns to an often-vulnerable group within the church: widows. He has in mind four different "kinds" of widows:

- Older widows without supporting family (v 4)
- Older God-fearing widows who have no relatives to support them (v 3, 5, 9-10)
- Older self-indulgent widows (v 6)
- Younger widows (v 11-15)

He also has different people in mind in terms of taking responsibility for widows: family (v 4, 8, 16), church (v 3, 16), and some widows themselves (v 13-14).

❓ *What is the best way to treat the widows in each group? Who bears responsibility for each group?*

Not all widows are the same—but Paul's concern is always the same: that Christians honour widows appropriately, and that Christian widows serve Christ appropriately.

⌄ Apply

❓ *Do verses 3-16 apply to you personally in any way? If so, how?*

❓ *Do you need to speak to a pastor or trusted Christian friend to talk through how you are being called to live, or to support someone else in your family or church?*

The heart of the matter

Proverbs talks a lot about "righteousness" and "wickedness". But what do these two words really mean?

❓ *What comes to your mind when you read those two words?*

If we look up these words in a standard dictionary, or think about how they are used in our culture, we end up with definitions that are about moral purity or extreme bad behaviour. But the Bible starts elsewhere: with the character of God. Righteousness is the quality of God's own perfection shown in his every attribute, every attitude, every thought, every behaviour and every word. Evil, or wickedness, is anything that falls short of this or runs counter to it.

Read Proverbs 11:19-21, 23

❓ *What warnings are given in these verses?*
❓ *What promises are given in them?*
❓ *What do they tell us about how God feels about the way humans live?*
❓ *How deep does the problem run?*
❓ *Why is this problematic for both God and us?*

God's laws both describe his own character and constitute the standard by which he measures human righteousness. It might just be possible to live a life externally that *seems* righteous to others—although it would be very difficult. But righteousness is active as well as passive—not just avoiding doing bad things but doing good, sacrificial, loving things. The line in the old Anglican Prayer Book Confession punctures any sense of moral achievement we may feel: "We have left undone those things which we ought to have done".

Once we throw our thoughts and hearts into the equation, then all is lost. This is the central problem in the Bible's story, which is only resolved with the death of the only person who ever lived a truly righteous life. This is the glorious good news of the gospel. "God made him who had no sin to be sin for us, so that in him we might become the righteousness of God" (2 Corinthians 5:21). When we place our trust in him, his righteousness becomes ours, and the Lord's anger at our perverse hearts turns to delight as he sees the righteousness of Christ in us. And that fuels us to live lives of righteousness ourselves, knowing that our God will see our righteous deeds and be pleased by them.

⌃ Pray

Praise God that, in Christ, he sees in you the perfection of his Son, and delights in you. Talk to the Lord about any false sense of your own righteousness you might have, and ask for help to let the righteousness of Christ shine through you today.

Over to you
Read Proverbs 11:22

As a man writing these notes, I can't possibly comment...

❓ *What point is the proverb seeking to make? How do you apply this in your own life?*

Elders and workers

Now Paul turns to how a church is to treat its "elders", and how Christians are to honour God in their work relationships.

Worthy of honour
Read 1 Timothy 5:17-25

❷ *How does verse 17 help us see what an elder's ministry is?*

❷ *What kind of elders is Paul speaking of (v 17)?*

❷ *What are they worthy of (v 17)? What do verses 18-21 suggest this involves?*

This is not an invitation to sit in judgment over our elders. We are to obey and submit to our leaders, for they are answerable to God and not to us (Hebrews 13:17). Such answerability to God does not excuse their responsibility to manage well—it heightens it. The worthiness of an elder is attached not to his position but to his quality of managing. And Paul says that those elders who toil at preaching and teaching the word are managing well and therefore worthy of double honour.

The "double" is usually taken to refer to both senses of the word "honour" or "value", i.e. honour and honorarium. More likely, though, the next few verses spell out the two honours due to such men. They are to be paid (v 18) and protected (v 19). In terms of protection, Paul knows leaders are always prone to being attacked. Their prominence makes them easy targets, and the easiest way to attack a message is to shoot the messengers. It is not as if leaders never fail, but the minimum standards of evidence must be strictly adhered to if justice is to be done.

❷ *How is Timothy to proceed if an accusation against an elder is:*
• *made?*   • *proved?*

The command to "reprove" in front of everyone indicates this is not about private sin.

❷ *Why is verse 21 so hard to obey when an accusation is made within the church?*

The warning against prejudging is paralleled with the command in v 22: "Do not be hasty in the laying on of hands". The context of the passage may be that of "appointing" elders or showing acceptance of repentant sinners (or both)—either (or both) is to be done thoughtfully and carefully.

Worthy of respect
Read 1 Timothy 6:1-2a

❷ *How should slaves treat masters? Why?*

This is not the place to go into the Bible's teaching on slavery. But these verses remind us that God calls us to fulfil our obligations.

❷ *What principles do you see here that apply to your own life?*

◣ Pray

Thank God for those who lead your church. Ask God to lead your church wisely in paying and protecting them well, and ask God to equip your leaders to teach you truth and exemplify the behaviour that flows from knowing Christ.

Contentment or disaster

Paul has already taken aim at the "austerity gospel" (4:1-5). Now, he sets his sights on the "prosperity gospel". They are opposite, but equally tragic and deadly, dangers.

Means to an end
Read 1 Timothy 6:2b-5

❷ *How does Paul describe those who "[do] not agree to the sound instruction of our Lord Jesus Christ" (v 3) in verse 4?*

"Godliness" (v 3, ESV) is all about what God has done for us in Christ Jesus. The false alternatives are all about what we have to do to be found acceptable to God. To be a teacher of such falsehoods requires somebody to have arrived (in their own estimation) at a superior position of perfection or enlightenment. There is always conceit involved in refusing to listen to Jesus.

❷ *What does the teaching of these false teachers result in (v 4b-5)?*
❷ *In what sense do they view being "godly" as a means to another end (v 5)?*

The key to contentment
Read 1 Timothy 6:6-10

❷ *What is truly a "great gain" (v 6)?*
❷ *How does v 7-8 show what Paul means by this type of attitude towards life?*

Paul is not saying that owning more than that is wrong in any moral sense (see v 17-19). But he is saying that the possessions of this world are only for this world. The key lies in contentment: in being content with reality. With contentment, we can abound or be brought low, face plenty or hunger and abundance or need, and give in to neither grasping nor bitterness (Philippians 4:12).

❷ *What does the alternative to this kind of contentment lead to (1 Timothy 6:9)?*

Wanting to be rich is a fairly dormant desire for those of us who have no realistic possibility of ever gaining great wealth. Yet the massive amount of money spent on gambling, or the obsession with wealthy celebrities indicates how easily our dormant desire can awaken into godless activity.

The emphasis of v 10 is "root". This is the explanation of v 9—how the desire to be rich leads to disaster. The love of money is not the full flower of our sin but a starting point upon which all of it grows and is fed.

⌃ Pray

It is very hard to discern our own hearts when it comes to contentment, possessions and wealth (or the desire for it). Ask God to show you your heart as it really is, so that you can grow in the "great gain" of "godliness with contentment".

⌄ Apply

❷ *Do you believe verse 10? How does this reveal itself in your own attitude to money?*
❷ *Is verse 8 true of you? How does this reveal itself in your attitudes to good things that you don't have?*

Pursuing and keeping

"Man of God" is an Old Testament term used of the leader of God's people. In the New Testament, it is used only by Paul to speak to Timothy.

And this man of God must do two things...

A God-given effort

Read 1 Timothy 6:9-12

> ❷ *What is "all this" from which Timothy must "flee" (v 11)?*
>
> ❷ *What does this require him to do, positively (v 11)?*

This is a short list—not by any means a comprehensive list—of the desires and aspirations to be pursued not only by Timothy but also by anyone who would be a faithful servant of God. We cannot achieve any of them solely by our efforts of pursuit—they are all the gifts of God. Yet we should pursue each of them, not the least by continual prayer for God to develop them in us and us in them.

> ❷ *What else must Timothy do (v 12)?*

This is a metaphor for the effort someone has to put in when teaching and living the truth.

⌃ Pray

No one grows as a Christian by accident. It requires our efforts and God's work (including his work in us to cause us to make that effort.)

> ❷ *Which of the desires and aspirations in verse 11 do you most need to "pursue"?*

Pray today, and each day, that God will equip you to make every effort to grow in this quality.

A command to keep

Read 1 Timothy 6:13-14

As in 5:21, the charge in 6:13 adds nothing to the logic of what Paul is saying, but raises the importance and significance of it. But what "this command" in verse 14 is, precisely, is unclear! Timothy is to flee evil and pursue righteousness, and he is to fight the good fight and take hold of eternal life. It could be all or any of these!

A reason to praise

Read 1 Timothy 6:15-16

Mention of the appearing of Jesus provokes an outpouring of praise to God. It is to this one and only God, who will display his Son again in his appearing, to whom Paul ascribes "honour and might for ever" (v 16). Who else would we want to rule us eternally?!

⌃ Pray

Spend time praising this God, who has made himself known through the gospel of his Son, and then recommit yourself to living a life of obedience to his commands and faithfulness in his cause.

Giving and guarding

Now Paul concludes his letter to Timothy with a final word for the rich and a final exhortation to his "true son in the faith" (1:2).

Give

Read 1 Timothy 6:17-19

❓ What are rich Christians not to be?

❓ What are they to do (v 17-18)?

❓ What motivation for living like this does verse 19 offer?

Here is the consistent temptation for people of wealth, especially in a materialistic meritocracy—to think of ourselves as important, above the rest, high and significant. It is the temptation of the self-made to worship their maker! Added to this arrogance is the blindness of assuming that wealth gives security for the future (v 17). But "wealth ... is so uncertain". At any time, the economy can be devalued or our particular wealth can be destroyed. We know that—but we tend to ignore it.

All of us—and especially if we have any wealth—need to learn that it is more blessed to give than to receive (v 18; see Acts 20:35). Like the former thief who is to no longer take but to work in order to give (Ephesians 4:28), the rich are to do good with their wealth. They are to be like God—generous. By sharing in this way the wealth that God has provided, the rich will be rightly using money for eternity. For though money is the currency of this world (1 Timothy 6:7), it can be used for eternity (v 19). True life is not to be found in wealth but in knowing Jesus and using our wealth in his service.

☑ Apply

❓ If someone else had a sight of your bank statement, would they think these verses should be a challenge to you, or an encouragement to you, or both? Why?

❓ In what sense do you need to hear the "command" here? What will change?

Guard

Read 1 Timothy 6:20-21

❓ What is Timothy to do, and what is he to take care not to do (v 20)?

Timothy has been entrusted with a great responsibility (1:18), and the whole letter instructs him in how—as one who knows the secret of godliness—he is to behave. His task has been to silence opponents by laying the truth of how to behave in the household of faith before the church. Guarding what has been entrusted to him requires avoiding the empty nonsense of false knowledge. This matters—for gospel faith leads to life, and following false teaching means departing from that faith (v 21).

⌃ Pray

Is there anyone you know who is swerving from the faith? Pray for them now, asking God to restore them to the gospel; and pray for yourself, that you might have opportunity to exhort them to return to faith in Christ, and him alone.

True godliness

As we finish our time in Paul's first letter to his "true son in the faith", Timothy, we're going to enjoy looking back over the letter as a whole.

So that you will know
Read 1 Timothy 3:14-16

- ❓ *Why was Paul writing to Timothy (v 14-15)?*
- ❓ *What great gospel truths are the foundation for the Christian life (v 16)?*
- ❓ *What "springs" from knowing the revealed "mystery" of God coming to us in Christ (v 16)?*

Prayer
Read 1 Timothy 2:1-8

- ❓ *What does a prayer life that springs from true godliness look like?*

Ministry
Read 1 Timothy 1:3-5; 4:6-16; 6:11-12

- ❓ *What does a ministry that springs from true godliness look like?*

Wealth and possessions
Read 1 Timothy 4:2-5; 6:6-10, 17-19

- ❓ *What does an attitude to good things in this world that springs from true godliness look like?*

Character
Read 1 Timothy 3:2-13

- ❓ *What does a character that springs from true godliness look like?*

⌄ Apply

- ❓ *What has most encouraged you in your time studying this letter?*
- ❓ *How has the Spirit been prompting you to change? Have you begun prayerfully to pursue that change?*
- ❓ *What one verse or passage would be useful for you to memorise?*

⌃ Pray

Use your answers to the Apply questions above to praise "God, the blessed and only Ruler, the King of kings and Lord of lords, who alone is immortal and who lives in unapproachable light" (6:15-16).

Using wealth well

Over a lifetime many of us will earn over a million; some will earn much more than that. How we use and steward this resource is a key part of righteous, godly living.

Generous returns
Read Proverbs 11:24-25

❷ What counter-intuitive principle is being brought to our attention here?
❷ How do you think this works in practical reality—even though it seems to make no economic sense?
❷ How does this principle relate to the character and nature of God?
❷ What are good and what are bad ways of applying this principle?

God is wonderfully generous. He is a loving Father, who showers us with good gifts day after day. Generosity is a thoroughly *good* thing, not just because it does good to others but because it does good to us. When we know that riches are not central to living "the good life", and that they are irrelevant for our status in eternity (see 11:4), it helps us to not become attached to them. The big danger with our possessions is that (as we've seen in 1 Timothy) they can come to possess us, ruling our hearts and minds.

The unspoken element in these verses is God himself. It is God who blesses—so when we turn our eyes to riches and away from God, it is no surprise that joy escapes us and that often poverty beckons.

···· TIME OUT ···

Read Matthew 6:24

❷ What is the danger when it comes to our money?

Refreshment
Read Proverbs 11:25-26

❷ What fresh aspect of wealth and generosity is brought into focus here?
❷ Why is this important to keep in mind?

We often default to thinking that morality is a personal thing. But Proverbs is always pointing us to remember that it is social, relational and spiritual. Our choices and attitudes deeply affect other people, bringing either joy and harmony or bitterness and division. How you think about and handle money affects everyone around you, for better or worse. This is not just about giving money away—it may involve selling something at a reasonable price to someone, even though you know you could get more elsewhere (v 26). For a New Testament example of this kind of refreshment through generosity, **read Philemon v 4-7.**

Apply

❷ Who do you know whose presence refreshes you in the sense that these verses speak of? What is it about them that brings this quality, do you think?
❷ How could you emulate them, refresh others, and so find refreshment yourself?

 Bible in a year: Deuteronomy 7-9 • Acts 2 v 22-47

The right pathway

"She's looking for trouble". "He's drawn to the dark side." We all have moments when our fallen hearts seek out things we know are ruinous to us. There's a better way…

Pathways
Read Proverbs 11:27

- ❓ *What twin promises do we read in verse 27?*
- ❓ *In what circumstances would this be a comforting verse? When would it be terrifying?*
- ❓ *What do you think is involved in seeking good in everyday life?*

If we are in Christ, our hearts and consciences have been renewed, and his Spirit lives in us to love good and hate what God hates. And yet there will still be times when our fallen nature fights back: when we're tired, or have had a disappointment, perhaps; or when we are not engaged in active serving; or sometimes even just after we have had a spiritual "high", like serving on a Christian holiday, sharing the gospel with a friend, or preaching.

⌄ Apply

- ❓ *When do you think you are most vulnerable to "searching for evil"?*
- ❓ *How do you think you can encourage yourself to seek good on a daily basis?*

⌃ Pray

Pray the Lord's Prayer (Matthew 6:9-13) and dwell on the line "Lead us not into temptation".

Planting and reaping
Read Proverbs 11:28-31

- ❓ *What agricultural images are brought out in verses 28 and 30?*
- ❓ *How do the blessings promised in these verses come to us?*
- ❓ *What is the idea in verse 31? To what extent do you see the truth of this around you?*

Fruitful flourishing is a metaphor used throughout the Bible to describe the good life that God created us for. It is at the heart of the concept of *shalom*—God's people living God's way with each other under God's generous blessing. It is what sin spoils and ruins. The love we are meant to give to others in relationship is turned in and spent on ourselves. Families break down; communities fracture; everyone loses. Verse 29 gives a graphic picture of this in family life.

We see these general principles of life played out around us all the time. Verse 31 reminds us that, in general, goodness brings its own rewards, as does unrighteousness. And when that does not seem to hold true in this world, there is a bigger picture that we must never forget: *eternity*.

⌃ Pray

Talk to the Lord about struggling families and wayward children you know.

Bible in a year: Deuteronomy 10-12 • Acts 3

CARING FOR YOUR PASTOR:
THE DIFFERENCE IT MAKES

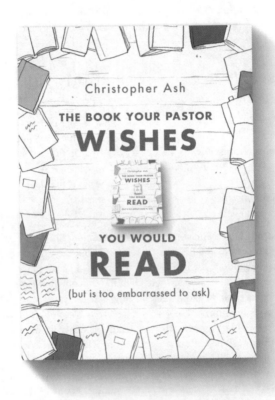

What do you think about your pastor? The truth is, often we think, "What can my pastor do for me?" Far less often do we think, "What can I do for my pastor?" Seasoned former pastor Christopher Ash urges us to remember that pastors are people and to pray for them as they serve us. Paradoxically, doing so will be a blessing to us as well as to them, as we create a culture of true fellowship in our church family.

thegoodbook.co.uk/wishes
thegoodbook.com/wishes

MISSION: YOUR PLACE IN GOD'S PLAN FOR THE NATIONS

These seven studies chart the unfolding of God's plan for
mission in the Scriptures. See God's loving concern for a lost
world, align your priorities with his, and get ready to play
your part in God's exciting plan for the nations.

**thegoodbook.co.uk/mission
thegoodbook.com/mission**

Introduce a friend to

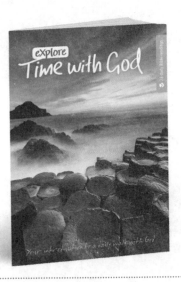

explore

If you're enjoying using *Explore*, why not introduce a friend? *Time with God* is our introduction to daily Bible reading and is a great way to get started with a regular time with God. It includes 28 daily readings along with articles, advice and practical tips on how to apply what the passage teaches.

Why not order a copy for someone you would like to encourage?

Coming up next...

❤ John 13–19
with Josh Moody

❤ Zechariah
with Carl Laferton

❤ Genesis 16–35
with Phil Allcock

❤ Proverbs
with Tim Thornborough